My friends Craig and Amy G ___ offers solid advice on creating a marriage that lasts. Whether you are considering marriage, remarriage, or simply want to strengthen your marriage, this book has something significant to offer.

— ANDY STANLEY, Senior Pastor, North Point Ministries

Craig and Amy Groeschel pour their hearts into this book. This beautiful couple provide inspiring advice on how to maintain a loving and strong marriage through faith, fun, trust, and love.

— MARK BURNETT AND ROMA DOWNEY

Every couple walks into marriage with expectations, but some couples are smart enough to recognize it. This book is a resource that I wish I'd had when I first got married, but I'm excited to share it with my friends! I'm so proud of Amy and Craig and their leading others to love well from this day forward.

— CHRISTINE CAINE, founder, The A21 Campaign; bestselling author, *Undaunted*

The definition of insanity is doing the same thing over and over but expecting a different result. If you want a better marriage, you've got to make some changes, starting with your expectations. Craig and Amy Groeschel give us all the wake-up call we need to safeguard our marriages against becoming another divorce statistic.

— DAVE RAMSEY, *New York Times* bestselling author and nationally syndicated radio show host

I cannot think of two better people to deliver such practical and potent truth about marriage. Craig and Amy Groeschel have a marriage that embodies the partnership, passion, love, and potential that God desires to birth in every couple. This book is for those seeking marriage and those already on the journey, with encouragement from voices that ring true with helpful advice that every reader can put into action from page one on. Get this book and start toward a stronger, happier marriage today.

— LOUIE GIGLIO, Passion City Church/Passion Conferences

Bobbie and I have a deep love and respect for both Craig and Amy Groeschel. Not only have we had the privilege of getting to know them personally, but also we have been able to observe their family and their ministry and found the fruit of their lives to be godly, full of wisdom, and contagiously joyful to be around. I have no doubt that their principles for a life of intimate marriage and commitment will refresh and inspire your relationship and give you practical tools as you seek God from this day forward.

— BRIAN HOUSTON, Senior Pastor, Hillsong Church

I'm a big fan of Craig Groeschel. His newest book, *From This Day Forward*, cowritten with his wife, Amy, is honest, entertaining, and optimistic. It's a shot in the arm for married couples. It's a thoughtful and instructive engagement gift. More than anything, it's a tell-it-like-it-is guide to a solid, lasting marriage. Read this book — and pass it on.

— KEN BLANCHARD, coauthor,
The One Minute Manager and *Lead Like Jesus*

FROM THIS
DAY FORWARD

Other Books by Craig Groeschel

Altar Ego: Becoming Who God Says You Are

Chazown: Define Your Vision, Pursue Your Passion,
Live Your Life on Purpose

The Christian Atheist:
Believing in God but Living as If He Doesn't Exist

Dare to Drop the Pose
(previously titled Confessions of a Pastor)

Fight: Winning the Battles That Matter Most

It: How Churches and Leaders Can Get It and Keep It

Love, Sex, and Happily Ever After
(previously titled Going All the Way)

Soul Detox: Clean Living in a Contaminated World

Weird: Because Normal Isn't Working

What Is God Really Like? (general editor)

FROM THIS DAY FORWARD

Five Commitments to Fail-Proof Your Marriage

CRAIG & AMY GROESCHEL

ZONDERVAN®

ZONDERVAN

From This Day Forward
Copyright © 2014 by Craig Groeschel

This title is also available as a Zondervan ebook.
Visit www.zondervan.com/ebooks.

Requests for information should be addressed to:

Zondervan, 3900 *Sparks Dr. SE, Grand Rapids, Michigan 49546*

ISBN 978-0-310-33384-5

Craig Groeschel is represented by Thomas J. Winters and Jeffrey C. Dunn of Winters, King & Associates, Inc., Tulsa, Oklahoma.

Cover design: *Curt Diepenhorst*
Cover photo: *Michelle Meisner*
Interior design: *Katherine Lloyd, The DESK*

First Printing August 2014 / Printed in the United States of America

Contents

WHAT DID YOU EXPECT?

When you were a child, did you ever wonder what marriage would be like one day? If you're a woman, did you ever fantasize about one day growing up and getting married in a perfect fairytale wedding? If you did, I'd be willing to bet that in your dream, your husband had movie star looks and flawless hair. When you started your fantasy life together, I'll bet he carried you across the threshold of your perfect house, a gorgeous home with beautiful shutters and a perfectly manicured lawn surrounded by all your favorite flowers.

And that amazing man of your dreams loved you like crazy. Together you had the ideal number of beautiful children, each one with just the perfect name. (Of course, you were too young then to pay attention to details like pregnancy weight gain, stretch marks, and C-sections.) In your beautiful dream, your family could have been models for those pictures that come with new picture frames.

Now, what about the guys? When you were a teenager, what did *you* dream about for your marriage?

Again, I'm just guessing, but I'll bet your wife looked pretty much like a bikini model. I'll bet she had blond hair (or whatever color's your favorite), if you even thought about details like that. In fact, I'll bet you couldn't tell me what color eyes your fantasy woman had. But I'll bet you were just sure you'd have sex at least twice a day — and three times on Sundays!

Now let me ask you, whether you're a woman or a man: Are you still dreaming? Or has reality set in for you?

Is your marriage what you expected it to be?

GREAT EXPECTATIONS

The truth is that all of us carry all sorts of expectations into marriage. We imagine what it might be like, constructing ideal circumstances. But then when marriage inevitably doesn't meet those expectations, many of us experience the crash: letdown, disappointment, pain, anger, frustration, despair — often even divorce. We wonder what went wrong when we thought we'd met Mr. or Mrs. Right. We wonder how we could've been so mistaken about this person we thought we wanted to spend our lives with.

But here's the hard truth about marriage: no one's expectations hold up. They're based on romantic fantasies and chick flicks and airbrushed images of perfect bodies and compliant attitudes. The harsh reality is that we're all imperfect human beings. Everybody occasionally forgets to put the toothpaste cap back on, or to lower or raise the toilet seat. Which is a reminder that everybody actually uses the bathroom.

Everybody wakes up with stinky morning breath. Everybody gets runny noses sometimes, and even diarrhea! It's gross, sure, but you know it's also true. Everybody loses their temper or says hurtful things from time to time. But strangely, those things never make the cut in those fantasies we imagine for ourselves, even though they're all just as true about *you* as they are about your spouse!

Maybe you've been wounded in past relationships. Maybe you've watched your friends, your parents, your adult children go through divorces. Maybe you're even in a relationship right now that you know is on life support. Because of your own experiences, you can't help asking yourself, "Is a good marriage even possible — let alone a *great* one?"

Call me crazy, but I believe with all my heart that, yes, it is possible to have a great marriage. Not just a healthy relationship but a loving, thriving, helping-each-other-reach-your-full-potential relationship. No surprise then that having this kind of marriage isn't easy. It takes work, and it takes specific kinds of work. The truth is you're not even likely to have a so-so marriage if you just keep doing the same things that everyone else is doing.

It's easy to see why this is true. Horrifying, heart-numbing statistics are easy to find — in magazines, on the internet, and even in the lives of our friends and families. About fifty percent of marriages don't make it. And if you're young, say under twenty-five, when you start your married life together, guess what? Your odds are even worse. And it doesn't matter how much money you make, how educated you are, what your ethnic background is, or whether you're a Christian. Statistically, it's a coin toss for almost everyone.

Even of the fifty percent or so who *do* stick it out, we know that a lot of those are miserable. They don't have any real intimacy. They feel unfulfilled in their lives and their dreams. A lot of couples just "stick together for the kids" or because they're afraid to be alone as a single parent. It seems like it's more and more common in the generation just ahead of mine to divorce later in life, once that last kid is out of the house.

No matter how you look at it, if you choose to get married, the odds are stacked against you. So take just a moment and think about this with me: in what other significant areas of your life are you willing to settle for fifty-fifty odds?

Let's say a news report comes out that fifty percent of the people who eat your favorite kind of breakfast cereal develop cancer. Let's imagine that researchers have even proven that it's the cereal causing it. Would you keep eating that same kind of cereal? Of course not! You'd try something different.

What if you got reliable information from an inside source that some economic news is about to come out that's guaranteed to cause widespread panic? In fact, if you just leave all of your investments in the market and all your savings in the bank, as soon as this report gets out, there's a fifty percent chance you're going to lose everything. What would you do? You'd freak out! You'd start asking questions. You'd spring into action as fast as you could. "What can I do? Is there someplace safe I can put my money?" You wouldn't just wait to see what happens.

What if you found out that an airborne virus is sweeping across the planet, infecting cats with a brain bug that makes them go crazy and eat their owners? If there were even just a fifty percent chance your cat could catch it, the next time you notice Fluffy glaring at you from his favorite sunny windowsill, you'd scoop up the nearest scratching post to defend yourself with and start planning your escape.

My point is when the odds are fifty-fifty in an area of your life that matters, you change your behavior. You don't just keep doing the same thing everybody else is doing. The results are obvious; they're all around you. You already know how that plays out. So why would you take a chance with your marriage? Wouldn't you want to find a better way and improve your odds?

Where I live, before you can get a license to drive a car, you have to take a class and pass a written test. And even after all of that, you *still* have to pass a driving test. Once you pass the test, you have to go wait at the DMV to pay another fee to get your license.

But if you want to get married, all you have to do is write a fifty-dollar check for a marriage license. No class, no written exam, no couples counseling, no conflict resolution seminars, no having to prove you have the slightest idea what you're getting yourself into. It's crazy that you can enter into what's supposed to be a lifelong commitment with zero preparation.

The truth is that in our culture today, most couples spend months and months planning and preparing for their wedding. They endlessly discuss and negotiate tiny details, like what color the type on the invitations should be and what kind of flowers to have, what kind of dress to wear and what food to serve at the reception. They expend hours and hours of time and effort and spend thousands of dollars. And yet these same two thoughtful people invest absolutely nothing in preparing for their *marriage relationship*. A successful wedding lasts maybe an hour (not counting the reception). You say that you want your marriage to last for the rest of your life, so doesn't it deserve at least the same forethought and attention to detail?

If you're not married yet, I have great news for you. There's still time for you to start right. You can learn how to do things differently than this world, differently than more than fifty percent of the couples around you. You're lucky. It's not too late to learn how to do things God's way. You can prepare for some of the hard stuff before it arrives on your doorstep. You can join with another person in a life that brings honor to God and to each other. You can build something together that's not just a legal arrangement, not just your signatures on a piece of paper, but a spiritual covenant before a holy God, a life of worship. If you put God first together, he will absolutely grant you the kind of marriage he wants you to have. He delights in doing it.

If you're already married, I have great news for you too. If you didn't get started off in the right way, it's not too late. Or even if you got started off right, but somewhere along the way you lost your footing, there's still hope. Have you ever seen those before-and-after videos of people who lost a bunch of weight after they committed to some workout program? How did that happen for them?

They quit doing the things they were doing before, and they started doing something different.

They traded their ice cream for running shoes and their donuts for dumbbells. They stopped eating by default and began eating to be healthy. They stopped channel surfing on the couch and began Zumba classes at the gym. If you're tired of resigning yourself to a mediocre marriage or a rocky relationship, you can take this same approach.

God's plans for your marriage still offer you hope and a new start. All you have to do is stop what you've been doing — those same things that everybody else does, those things that lead to fifty percent or more of marriages failing — and start living his best for your marriage.

FROM THIS DAY FORWARD

My wife, Amy, and I don't have a perfect marriage — far from it. But we love each other more now than when we said "I do" more than twenty-three years (and six kids) ago. We've discovered that the key to a successful marriage is something you've heard before. But you may not have thought about what it means. Your key to a joyful, life-giving marriage begins with your completely understanding this one simple phrase: "I, [your name here], take you, [your spouse's name here], to have and to hold, *from this day forward*."

Those four little words are packed full of hope, brimming with promise: "From this day forward."

What happened in your past doesn't matter. Did you mess up when you were dating? That's okay! Have you struggled with communicating? That's okay! Have you said things you wish you could take back? That's okay! Have you done things you regret? *It's okay.* God's mercies, his compassions, never fail. They are new every morning. And he is always faithful (Lam. 3:22 – 23).

Draw a line at today. Your new lifelong love life, your new love affair with each other, the greatest marriage you can imagine, begins now. Today. From this day forward. Right now, in this very moment, you can commit that everything that happens from now on will represent your sacred commitment to your spouse before a holy God.

"From this day forward."

A lot of people seem to ignore the fact that, if you've chosen to follow Christ, regardless of whether it was before or after you slipped that ring onto that special someone's finger, it's a commitment you make before God. It's easy to excuse our own behavior — our mistakes and bad habits — when we compare our shortcomings with our spouse's. But for those of us who call ourselves Christians, that's not really our standard, is it?

We say, "I take you for better or for worse, for richer or for poorer, in sickness and in health, and forsaking all others, I will be faithful to you for as long as we both shall live, *so help me, God.*"

I think the problem for a lot of us is that we say that last part in a monotone voice, like it's some kind of pledge we memorized in school, like we're about to be cross-examined in traffic court: "so help me, God."

Instead, we need to think of it as a request to the only one who can save us: "I'm deciding to do all of these things, and I really, *really* mean it. So *please!* Help me, God!"

17

When we think of it in this way, we allow God to take his rightful place in our relationships. We acknowledge our weaknesses, admitting that we know it's impossible for us to keep our commitments unless we choose to honor him at the very center of our marriage (2 Cor. 12:9). Our commitment to each other is mirrored in our holy covenant before him.

And our commitments are based on decisions. The choices you make each and every day determine not only your relationship with God but also the quality of your marriage. The decisions you make today determine the marriage you will have tomorrow. In this book, Amy and I would like to share with you five decisions that will fail-proof your marriage. If you make these decisions, you can and will have the marriage God wants you to experience.

So what I'm asking you to do here — in fact, what I'm *daring* you to do — is to decide to do these five things in your marriage:

1. Seek God.
2. Fight fair.
3. Have fun.
4. Stay pure.
5. Never give up.

If you and your spouse (or future spouse) earnestly choose to do all five of these things, I promise you'll discover a richer, deeper, more authentic, more rewarding, more passionate love life than the greatest fantasy your teenage self ever could have imagined.

Don't be a statistic. Don't be average. Let's get you that marriage that you always wanted.

Starting right now, from this day forward.

SEEK GOD

"God, the best maker of all marriages,
combine your hearts into one."
— William Shakespeare, Henry V

In our culture, everybody knows about "the one."

Romantic comedies, "successful" celebrity relationships, online dating sites, even most of our friends, are constantly repeating this message: "All you have to do to be genuinely fulfilled is to find 'the one.' Once you do, everything will be rainbows and hearts and flowers and love songs from then on."

So even as Christians, we spend a lot of time before marriage searching for that one perfect soul mate. We even reinforce our quest with Scripture. You're probably familiar with that "seek and you will find" verse. You know, the one in Matthew 7:7 – 8 where Jesus says, "Ask and it will be given to you; seek and you will find; knock and the door will be opened to you. For everyone who asks receives; the one who seeks finds; and to the one who knocks, the door will be opened."

You may even have it memorized. If you're a single follower of Christ still looking for that special someone, maybe you even pray it every day with genuine sincerity: "Jesus, you said I could ask for whatever I want and it will be given to me. You said that if I seek, I'll find, and that if I ask, I'll receive. So Lord, this is me asking: Please send me that person who will complete me. You *promised*. So now you have to do it! Also, thanks. Amen."

I mean, everybody knows that you can't truly be happy in this life until you've met "the one," right? If you're a Christian who's not yet married, you've probably already been seeking that one person who you're just certain can meet your needs. They're your future spouse — they just don't know it yet. And if you're married, all you want is for the spouse you already have to just step up once and for all and meet all those needs you expected them to. (Why are they so stubborn, anyway? Why won't they just do what you want so you can finally be happy?)

You know the story: Boy meets girl. Boy sees girl is pretty. Boy notices that girl's hair smells good. Boy's mind is blown. "She's the one!"

Of course, girls are much more sophisticated than that.

She starts a mass text exchange with all her girlfriends immediately after that first magical date: "OMGosh! So sweet! His eyes are amazing and you can tell he works out!" And what's the one thing they *always* say? "We just talked and talked and talked for hours! It felt like we could talk forever!" (Enjoy that while it lasts, ladies.) "He completes me. I just know he's the one!"

If you're already married, maybe you've prayed that same Bible verse, only slightly modified: "Jesus, you said I could ask for anything I wanted, and that if I asked, I'd receive. I honestly thought this person you sent me was the one. Now I'm not so sure anymore. But I'm asking you: Please change my spouse into the person I know they *could* be, someone who can complete me. I sure hope you're listening. Amen."

Usually, even when you think you've found "the one," it doesn't take long to question whether he or she really is the one. Things seemed to go well enough at first but then began to unravel. In the long run, finding that special one seems as impossible as panning for gold in the ocean. Why is that? Why does the one never seem to really be the one we were looking for?

I'm convinced there's a simple reason. While it's true that you *do* need to find that "one" to be truly complete, another *person* can never be "the one."

Just once I would love to hear somebody say, "I just met someone awesome and godly! We have so much fun together.

We have this amazing spiritual bond. You know, I think I might have just met 'the two!'" Why? Because to really be fulfilled in life, you do have to meet the One.

Here's the catch: God is your One. Your spouse is your two.

YOUR ONE AND ONLY

If you can get this, I honestly believe it's one of the most important foundational principles you need to maintain any meaningful, lasting relationship: God is your One.

But don't just take my word for it. Let's look at what Jesus said. In Matthew 22:36, a Pharisee (an expert in Hebrew law), asked Jesus, "Which is the greatest commandment?"

Jesus didn't answer, "Hey, that's easy! Love your spouse with your whole heart and soul." No. What *did* He say?

"Jesus replied, 'Love the Lord your God with all your heart and with all your soul and with all your mind.' ... And the second [most important commandment] is like it: 'Love your neighbor as yourself'" (Matt. 22:37, 39).

What Jesus was saying is essentially, "God is your One. Make him your One."

God is your One. Your spouse is your two.

Throughout this book, I'll be addressing both single people and married people (more about Amy's contribution at the end of this chapter). For now, we're going to start with those who aren't married but who would like to be one day. (Why? Because all the older married people always say, "I wish I had known that *before* I got married.")

Usually, when I address the single people at my church, I have them raise their hands. Then I have them look around and see if there's anybody else with their hand raised that they might consider a possibility. I really hope that one day, say, nineteen or twenty years from now, I start getting graduation announcements from kids at my church named Craig because I helped their parents find each other.

If you're not married yet, but you hope to be one day, I'd like you to commit to this. I suggest you even write it down and maybe tape it on the mirror in your bathroom or in your car, just someplace you'll see it every day: "I will seek the One while I prepare for my two."

If you're not married and you follow Christ, then above anything else, you should honor God. You should love him, seek him, get to know him, seek to please him, and live by his Spirit. You should structure your life so that everything you do brings glory to God. Don't seek a spouse. Instead, seek God's kingdom and his righteousness. When you do that first, according to Matthew 6:33, God will give you everything else you need.

The challenge is that a lot of the single people who consider themselves Christians in our culture today believe they can just put off "the God thing" until they're older. They figure they'll have plenty of time to focus on that later in life, convincing themselves that those things don't really matter much while they're young.

Single people often seem to think, "One day I'll get married, and then I'll get my family in on that whole church thing. But for now, I really just want to have some fun. I'm going to hit a few clubs and try to meet lots of different people. Sure, I might be jumping around from person to person now — and maybe some people might even consider my life sort of shallow or 'ungodly' or whatever — but I can always take care of my spiritual business later." This lifestyle attitude has become quite common, and it's incredibly dangerous, preventing you from finding the kind of person you truly want to marry.

SOMEONE LIKE YOU

Andy Stanley is a pastor at a really great church, and he's also a close friend of mine. I heard Andy tell a story once that I feel illustrates this better than I ever could. Here's my version of his story:

There was this young girl, a very committed Christian. When she went away to college, she did what a lot of college students do. First, she gave in a little to some peer pressures. She started going to parties and mingling. What started as having a drink every now and then gradually melted into more and more. After a while, she tried a few drugs here and there too. Of course she met a lot of guys, which kind of evolved into guy after guy after guy after guy. Then, without really even realizing what was happening to her, she gradually slid into a lifestyle of very destructive sin.

Even as all of this was going on, somewhere in the back of her mind, she kept thinking, "I still believe in God. I'd still like to have a godly marriage one day. Sometime, I'll go back and do what I know is right." But in the meantime, she continued right on living her destructive lifestyle.

As fate would have it, one day a friend of hers introduced her to a guy out in front of the student union. He was everything she had ever hoped for in a potential husband: He was a godly, terrific leader. He even discipled other young men! He was already using his gifts to try to make a difference in the world, and he was just beginning what looked like was going to be a very promising career. She felt like they really hit it off, and she talked to him every chance she got.

After a few weeks, she was home one weekend, and she told her mom, "I'm pretty excited. I've met this guy at school. He's everything I ever wanted. He's godly and kind and wise. He's just perfect! He's exactly the kind of guy I've always wanted to marry. I think he might be the one for me, Mom. I'm thinking about letting him know how I feel."

The girl's mom frowned a little. As lovingly as she could, she said, "Oh, sweetheart, if this boy is everything you say he is, I think you really need to be honest with yourself: a young man like that probably isn't looking for a girl like you."

You know what's probably the worst thing about a story like this? That you know it's true! Here's a very simple principle you can take to the bank: It doesn't matter what you *want*; like attracts like. If you hope to have a godly marriage one day, you need to start living a godly life today.

Become the kind of person you would like to marry.

If the kind of person you want is someone who's had eighteen different sex partners, then by all means, go right ahead and be that person yourself. Only remember: If you do the same things everybody else does, your odds of a lasting marriage will be about the same as everybody else's: fifty-fifty. Your odds of a meaningful marriage will be much less. If you want something different from what everybody else has, then you're going to have to do something different than what everybody else does.

If you want a spouse who's sold out to Christ, then you need to devote yourself to Christ. If you want someone who seeks God daily in every area of their life, then you need to start pursuing God daily. If you're single and you want to be married one day, become the kind of person you would like to marry.

I will seek the One while I prepare for my two.

MARRIAGE MATH

Now, if you're already married, you need to pursue a different commitment: I will always seek the One with my two.

Why is this so important? Because our marriages will never be what God wants them to be unless we make him our One and we make our spouses our two. Unfortunately, a lot of us get those mixed up. Some people try to make their spouses the One. "I made you my everything. It's all on you now: make me happy!"

I know a few married people who are actually pretty good at making God their One, but then they put something besides their spouse into their number two spot. Some make their children their number two. Others make their careers their number two. But the only combination that works for marriage is to make God the One and your spouse the two.

When you try to make your spouse (or your boyfriend or girlfriend) the One, you're putting undue pressure on them. In fact, we have a word for when you raise another human being to that lofty position: idolatry. The truth is no person could ever be capable of meeting your needs. Mark Driscoll, in his book *Who Do You Think You Are?* writes, "Our idols always fail us, and eventually we end up demonizing the people we idolize" (pp. 192–93). When you idolize someone and then they let you down — which is inevitable, by the way, because every human makes mistakes and every human sins — then you're going to end up demonizing them. "How could you do that to me? Why won't you just meet my needs the way I need you to? Why are you so mean and selfish?"

We've all seen this before. When they first get together, your buddy tells you, "I love it that she's so organized. She's just so … so … driven. And I *love* it that she's so passionate about everything." Then, after they've been married for a while, time and experience gives him a slightly different perspective. "She's a control freak! She always has to have everything her way. Nothing I do is ever good enough for her. Her constant nagging drives me crazy." First we idolize; then we demonize.

Women experience the same thing, of course. She tells her friends, "You know the greatest thing about him? He's just so laid back. You know how I'm usually wound up so tight? Well, his chillness is just, like, the perfect complement to my personality. Being around him soothes me, you know? He comforts me." But then once she's had some time to settle in, those very things she used to find charming about him start eating away at her. "He's such a bump on a log! I can never get him to go out. He never wants to do anything. And he just refuses to lead our family. I'm pretty sure he'd be happiest if I'd just let him sit in his recliner and play video games all day, every day." When we start out idolizing another person, it's inevitable: we'll wind up villainizing them at some point.

That's why, when you're married, you need to fix your resolve: I will always seek the One with my two.

KEYSTONE HABITS

What does that even mean — to seek the One, to "seek God"? What are some practical ways we can pursue him, learn about him, and get to know him personally? When I started putting together ideas to teach this at our church, I ended up with what I was convinced was a great list. It was genuine. It included a bunch of things that my wife, Amy, and I do together to make sure we keep God as our One. And most of the things on my list weren't just practical; they were even really spiritual! Here's just a sample of what I put together, a list of ways that I believe couples should seek God together:

- Read God's Word together.
- Worship together regularly in a church and also in your home.
- Engage with friends who follow Christ in a small group setting that meets regularly.
- Ask your friends to hold both of you accountable to grow together spiritually.
- Use your gifts to serve together in church.
- Work together to make a difference in your community.

- Lead your children toward eternal values.
- Develop spiritual traditions together and with your children.

You can see for yourself: it was a great list! (And I've only shared part of it with you; I had a lot more.) But as I was praying about my ideas, I really felt that God was showing me that if I asked people to do eight things — or ten things or twelve things — chances are pretty good that most people would actually do *zero* of those things. Unfortunately, that's just the reality of being a pastor — or honestly, any kind of leader.

I decided that instead I just needed to talk about one simple thing. If what you want is to have a genuine relationship with God, the single most important spiritual discipline you need is to seek him.

That's pretty vague, so I know people can interpret it all sorts of different ways. Let me explain what I'm talking about. I recently read a book called *The Power of Habit* by Charles Duhigg. (Yes, pastors do read books besides the Bible.) In his book, Duhigg talks about something he calls *keystone habits*. Keystone habits are habits that, once you start doing them, create forward momentum that leads you to other good habits. Unfortunately, these same keystone habits — if you *don't* do them — can create negative momentum that will pull you toward negative habits. I've had the opportunity to teach on this topic at leadership events and conferences several times now, so I have this principle distilled to one simple piece of advice: "Never quit flossing."

FLOSSED AND FOUND

I know what you're thinking, and no, your dentist didn't call me and ask me to tell you that. It's actually much simpler. You have to figure out what your keystone habit is — that one thing that, if you stop doing it, is the catalyst that starts you sliding toward other bad habits. For me, flossing is the first discipline to go. If I stop flossing, it's inevitable: I'm going to start skipping workouts here and there. And when I skip a few workouts, inevitably, I'm going to end up eating something unhealthy.

Flossing, exercising, and watching what I eat are all really good disciplines that I've put into practice over time. And for whatever reason, they all seem to build on one another, like blocks in a pyramid. If I let one of these habits crumble, it sets off a chain reaction. They just start falling like dominoes, one after another.

But when I floss, I don't skip workouts. And when I exercise regularly, when I see food that tempts me, I think, "I'm going to say no to this right now. I've invested too much work into my exercise to sabotage it with this junk food. It's just not worth it to waste all of that effort."

When I floss, I exercise. When I exercise, I eat better. When I exercise and eat well, that makes me sleep better. When I sleep well, even though I wake up earlier, I feel refreshed. When I wake up early and feel good, I'm more focused, and I'm more productive during the day. When I feel like I'm doing everything God has called me to do, that makes me feel happy and fulfilled. Then when I go home at the end of the day, I don't feel like I left anything undone, so my work doesn't keep lingering in my mind.

Without work lingering in my mind, I'm free to give my attention to Amy and to our kids. And as I mentioned, we have six kids, so I have to stay really present to make sure there's enough of Daddy to go around. When the girls get enough talking and snuggling and smiling and affirmation from me, and when the boys get enough wrestling and tickling and noogies, all the kids are happy. And when I'm a good dad to our kids, that makes Amy feel really good about me. And when Amy feels really good about me ... well, let's just say flossing every single day is totally worth it!

On the other hand, if I don't floss, it's inevitable that I'll skip a workout. When I skip a workout, there's always leftover cupcakes or doughnuts or something at the office, and I figure, "Well, I didn't work out today, so I'm already off my routine. I'm just going to take today as a cheat day." So I finish the box. Later that evening, because I didn't work out and my energy is still erratic from the sugar high, when I go to bed, I'm restless and I don't sleep well.

When I go to work the next day, somebody mentions, "You've got dark circles under your eyes. And are you putting on weight?" So I'm disappointed in myself, and my disappointment evolves quickly into anger. I'm fuming as I'm driving home, so I'm speeding. When a police officer tries to pull me over, I make a run for it. There's a chase with helicopters and it's on TV, so then everybody in the whole city knows what happened. Of course, the police catch me and take me in for fleeing and for resisting arrest. And now, I'm writing this from my jail cell. And why?

All because I stopped flossing!

Never. Quit. Flossing.

SAY A LITTLE PRAYER

Of course I'm exaggerating here (a little), but it's to prove an important point. Some habits create forward momentum in your life. Those same habits, if you don't diligently keep them, create negative momentum. But I believe there's one keystone habit that, if you can do it consistently, will help you always diligently seek God. Even better, it's simple! If you'll do just this one thing every day, I can guarantee it will change your life: seek God together in prayer.

If you're a Christian married woman reading this, I imagine it probably made you giddy to read that just now. "Hurray! Yes! Now he *has* to pray with me!" But if you're a husband reading this, and you haven't already been praying with your wife, you might be groaning inside. "I don't mind praying, I just don't like to pray with *other people*. Not even with her. I never know what to say. Then it just gets ... awkward."

I promise I'll address all of that in just a minute. But first, I want to talk again to those of you who are not married but want to be one day. If you haven't prayed together with someone else before, I have to warn you: praying together is extremely intimate. When you join hands with another person, especially someone you might be attracted to, and you petition God together, asking him to do things on your behalf, I can't describe just how familiar, close, and bonding an experience that can be. If you have someone you're committed to, someone you're serious about, someone you would honestly consider marrying, while I think it's important that you pray together, I think it's equally important that you first set some safeguards and boundaries.

What I'm going to share with you here isn't in the Bible; it's just sound advice. Don't pray alone together in intimate settings where "things" could happen. (You know what "things" I mean.) Instead, pray in settings where you can be accountable, like with other friends present. Or pray together over the phone. Or pray together in a park, somewhere out in the open. Or pray together at a restaurant, where there's a big table separating you. Don't pray together alone on a sofa. And whatever you do, for God's sake, keep vertical. Never pray together on a bed. Don't try to pray horizontally! If you do that, you're just *asking* for trouble and impurity, and you *know* it. Trust me on this. Keep your prayer together as pure and spotless as you want your marriage to be.

Now, if you are married, of course it's fine for you to pray together in bed. (In fact, I recommend it.) It's good for your marriage. When you share a connection with God together, that will just naturally make you want to share other things together too.

Why is praying together so important? Well, 2 Chronicles 7:14 says, "If my people, who are called by my name, will humble themselves and pray and seek my face and turn from their wicked ways, then I will hear from heaven, and I will forgive their sin and will heal their land." Especially if you've already been facing challenges in your marriage, this is so important. If you will humble yourselves and pray and seek God's face, then I honestly believe that he will hear from heaven and he will heal your marriage.

START WHERE YOU ARE

Any time I teach about prayer, or even when I just talk to someone about it casually, I hear the same things over and over:

"I just don't know how!"

"I never know what to say."

"It just feels so awkward, so unnatural."

I hear you! But you know what? All of these things are true about anything you haven't done before. Throwing a baseball. Driving a car. Starting a new job.

I have four daughters, and I can remember struggling sometimes when they were little to brush their hair into perfect ponytails. It seems like every time I tried, they were always crooked, or not tight enough, or some cluster of rogue hairs would make a break for it and escape at the last minute. To this day, it leaves me in awe when I see one of them pinch a ponytail holder in her lips, lift her hair with both hands, stroke it back two or three times, grab it with one hand, and then with the other — *one-handed* — execute a flawless ponytail. Every time!

Just starting is the hard part.

I sincerely don't know how couples who don't follow Christ make it in this life. I don't know how two people can make it without seeking God.

I believe with all of my heart that our inability to pray together is a snare set by our enemy, Satan. He'd like nothing better than for none of us ever to seek God — not on our own, and certainly not with our two. What better way to steal our marriages from us, kill our love for one another, and in the process, destroy our families?

Pick somewhere and just start. For example, the next time you sit down to a meal, just say, "Hey, before we eat, I think I'd like to pray." Thank God for your food and ask him to help you get to know him better. "Amen!" Get in and get out! Or before you and your spouse head your different ways in the morning, do something Amy suggested: grab their hand and say, "God, please bless my spouse today. Please draw us closer to you and to each other." It doesn't matter where you start. All that matters is *that you start.*

Because some people get stuck and feel awkward during a prayer, maybe you should make a list of a few things you want to talk to God about. Keep it with you. Anytime you think of another thing, just add it to your list. Some possible categories might be your kids (present or future), decisions you need to make, your finances, or other people you want to pray for (sickness, family problems, job situation, whatever). When you have a few minutes, waiting for the subway or picking up your kids in carpool or something, pull out your list and just talk to God about two or three things on it. Tell him what's bothering you about each thing, and ask him if there's anything you should do about it. Ask him to intervene in some way.

If you think of something you'd like someone else to pray for you about, here's an idea: *ask.* You don't have to make it weird or put pressure on them. Just ask them to send you a quick text prayer or email prayer sometime when they have a few minutes. It really is that simple. (Of course, if you're married, this person should be your spouse.)

If you're married, when you have some time together, after the kids are all in bed and before you go to sleep at night, or before the kids are up when you're getting ready in the morning, take out your list and pray together for a few things on it. Keeping a list can seriously help you get past those awkward silences that conspire to strangle your new prayer habit.

With just a little practice, in no time at all, you can become a master of prayers of encouragement. I can't tell you how many times I've gotten a text from Amy out of the blue that said something like, "Praying God gives u peace today! Luv u!" You'd be amazed how much spiritual intimacy such a small thing builds between us. In fact, because of this, I'm convinced that couples praying together is a keystone habit.

Follow my logic here: When you pray together regularly, you're more likely to go to church together. If you go to church together regularly, you're probably going to get involved in serving at church together. When you serve together, you're going to meet more likeminded people at church. When you meet more people at church, you'll likely start spending time together with them outside of church too. That means you'll probably end up praying for them, and they'll pray for you.

And when you're praying for other people, and other people are praying for you, the next time someone cuts you off in traffic, you'll be far more likely to just laugh it off. (Maybe even — *gasp!* — *forgive* them and pray for *them!*) My point is that once you start developing the positive keystone habit of praying together, that will create positive spiritual momentum that will pay huge dividends in building up your marriage and other relationships.

FROM THIS PRAY FORWARD

I've already told you about all kinds of reasons you need to do this. Still another benefit is that when you seek God together — and especially once you see God answering those prayers — it builds your faith. But even if all of these "spiritual" things haven't convinced you yet, how about a few practical reasons?

It's really hard to fight with someone you pray with regularly. You really can't get into the whole drama of, "You're such a jerk! I can't stand you! You only think of yourself!" when just a few hours ago you were praying together for a friend whose child has cancer. When you're pursuing consistent, spiritual intimacy, you're a lot less likely to click on that porn ad on the internet, or to start an "emotional affair" by returning a coworker's flirtatious advances. Things change. *You* change. You start getting to really know God and what he's about. You start serving him with your life. And when those traps pop up that ensnare so many other marriages (oh, say, fifty percent or so), you spot them immediately and you shut them down.

Finally, here's one last one: Imagine how hard it must be to divorce someone you're genuinely seeking God with. What are the odds that God's direction to you is going to be, "Yeah, you should just split up"? Not likely.

If all of this is just too much for you, I guess I understand. You can just take your chances. The odds are at least fifty percent against you. And even if you do make it, chances are pretty good you're just going to be "sticking together for the kids," toughing it out for your whole life. If that's the life you want, of course that's your business. More power to you.

Me? I don't like those odds. I'd rather get crazy spiritual. I'd rather have people think my family's goofy and weird. They can think whatever they want. And in the meantime, together we'll enjoy a deep, rich, passionate marriage and family life. Amy and I are in agreement on this. We want to genuinely cry out to our One together: "So help us, God! Please help us! We want you involved in our everyday lives. We're going to come talk to you together — every day, all day."

A few years ago, an organization called Family Life surveyed thousands of Christian couples. Sadly, they discovered that fewer than eight percent of Christian couples said they prayed together regularly. Fortunately, their study also had some silver lining: of that eight percent of couples who pray together, fewer than one percent of them divorce.

So here's what that means to you: Go ahead and be just

like everybody else if you want. Do what everybody else does. Don't pray together. And your chances of making it will be about fifty-fifty. Or be different. Be like that eight percent. Pray together regularly. And increase your chances of making it to ninety-nine percent.

The choice is yours.

Matthew 6:33 tells us to "seek first [God's] kingdom and his righteousness, and all these things will be given to you as well."

We should seek God first. "So help us, God!" Maybe you haven't been doing that. Then you can start doing it "from this day forward."

That means we should be people of prayer. Maybe you don't feel like you know how to pray. That doesn't matter. Start doing it "from this day forward."

We should be centering all of our relationships around God, seeking him through prayer and through his Word. Maybe you haven't been getting along. Maybe you don't like each other very well right now. The hardest part is always starting. Get over your excuses. Start going before God "from this day forward."

So I challenge you, right now, to pray. Pray by yourself and pray with your spouse. Pray aloud if you're comfortable doing so. There's nothing magical about the words in the following sample prayer, but I thought they might help get you started. Add your own words, too, where you need to. But just pray.

Father, thank you that you love me. Thank you that you chose me to be your child. Help me to love you with all my heart, with all my soul, with all my strength, and with all my mind. Please show me how to make you my One. I will seek you first. Please help me to start and to keep the habit of seeking you. Please remind me to come to you over and over again, every day.

Father, thank you for my two. Please draw us both closer to you, and closer to each other. Please change my heart and change my mind. Make me the person that you want me to be. Make me the best two for my two that I can be. Every time I notice a "splinter" in my two's eye, please help me to immediately see the "log" that's in my own eye. Please give me the humility to pray, to seek your face, and to turn from my sins. Please hear me, and forgive me, and heal my relationships.

Thank you for loving me. Thank you for healing me. And thank you for empowering me to live in a way that glorifies you. In Jesus' name, amen.

You know what you need to do next. Starting is the hard part. So get the hard part over with: start. Then just keep right on going, together, every day, from this day forward.

AMY'S ANGLE

When I (Craig) am teaching about relationships at our church, it's important to me that I always involve Amy and ask her for her thoughts and feelings. I want whatever relationship advice I offer to include a woman's perspective. When I was preparing this book, I asked Amy to share what she feels is important for couples to know about each of the five decisions—seeking God, fighting fair, having fun, staying pure, and never giving up. Here's what she had to say about praying together.

You know that old saying, "Variety is the spice of life"? Well, that's just as true about prayer as it is about anything else. While it's important that couples pray together regularly, the temptation you're going to face is that it can just become routine, one more box you check during your day. When Craig and I were dating, and even after we first got married, we set mealtimes as regular opportunities for prayer.

We'd pray not just for our food but for anything else that we needed to talk to God about. Those prayers would often last for ten minutes or more! Our food got cold but our hearts got warmer.

As our lifestyle changed over time—Craig started seminary, we started having kids, we started the church, and so on—of course life got considerably busier. Long prayers at every meal just became impractical. So we adapted and found other times. We realized that what is important for us is that we make it a point to rely constantly on God's direction for whatever is going on in our lives.

Now Craig and I pray together almost every day and in a variety of ways. Fortunately, this approach keeps our prayers fresh and authentic, never just what the Bible calls "vain repetitions." Anytime something comes up that we need to address together in prayer, we try to make that happen as close to that moment as possible.

With technology, we have all sorts of ways to do that that didn't even exist before. He's busy with the church during the day, and I'm busy with our family and other commitments. But I know I can always text or email him, "Would you please pray with me for [blank]?" He'll always pray right away, or call me when he has a few minutes, and we'll pray together over the phone.

That works both ways, of course; Craig asks me to pray specific things for him all the time too: direction on an important decision, favor before a big meeting, or if he's starting to feel tired or sick or something. Maintaining that constant connection not only feeds our relationship and our love for one another, but it keeps our lives centered on our mutual trust in God, and our love for him.

You know what the hardest part about learning to pray together is? Starting. Seriously! You have to determine to lean into your relationship with God; simply start talking to him as your Father. You just tell him what you're feeling, what you need, and what you want. You express gratitude to him for the things he's already done, and you train your mind to continually trust and love him. Most of us make prayer so much more complicated than it needs to be. God never intended for prayer to intimidate us. He loves us so much that he adopted us as his own children, by his own choice. We're simply engaging in conversation with a Father who already loves us, talking to him about all the things that matter to us.

Keep it simple. Make what you say natural and honest. You can grab hands right before you head out the door for work and just say something aloud like,

"Father, thank you for this new day you've given us. Please lead us today into every opportunity that you want us to engage in." That's it! Don't think that you need to make it all fancy, sprinkling it with "thees" and "thines" or even "amens."

Now, if you want to pray together about something specific, you might want to organize your thoughts by writing them down. Sharing these written prayer requests with your spouse can really deepen your relationship.

Praying together is a little bit different to me than one of the habits Craig has already mentioned like, say, flossing, because that's something you probably do only once a day. Praying is more like breathing to me and Craig. It's constant, short bursts whenever the inspiration or need comes to us. And praying together should be the same way. Any need that has to do with Craig, I automatically involve him in it. With only a few minutes (or even seconds) scattered throughout the day, we share an open line of communication with each other and with God.

You *can* do this. Don't make it harder than it has to be, and stop putting it off. What do you have to lose by starting today? And more important, just think of all that you stand to gain.

FIGHT FAIR

A happy marriage is the union
of two good forgivers.
— Ruth Bell Graham

When Amy and I were still newlyweds, we soon clashed over one of the fundamental, most sacred aspects of any godly relationship: pancakes. Yeah, you read that right. Pancakes. That initial skirmish became the first of many epic battles in the most protracted war of wills recorded in the Groeschel marital history books. When I explain what happened, though, I think you'll understand why this wasn't just any old pancake war.

The sad reality is that my beautiful wife — although perfect in almost every other way and by no fault of her own — was raised in a dysfunctional pancake home (DPH). Her side of the family simply never learned how to make pancakes correctly. If you were brought up in good circumstances, by parents blessed with the spiritual gift of pancake making, then you'll understand. You make a relatively thin batter, turn the griddle up high, and get some butter sizzling on it. Then you pour only four pancakes, each one about four inches across, uniformly sized, and as close to perfect circles as possible.

Since you waited, of course, until the griddle had reached an appropriate temperature, the cakes bubble up quickly. You need to wait only a few seconds, and when the Spirit prompts you, you rapidly flip them at precisely the perfect moment. After a few more seconds, you stack those perfectly formed, perfectly browned pancakes quickly onto a waiting plate. You immediately apply butter (uniformly, naturally) in between layers and on top while the stack is still steaming, too hot to touch. Then drown the whole pile with authentic Log Cabin syrup. (If you want to see what pancakes are *supposed* to look like, it's easy to find proper pictures of them on the internet. But as always, please be sure you have "safe search" turned on and be sure not to accidentally type in "hotcakes.") Finally, you devour them while they're still hot, enjoying a momentary taste of what will be served each morning in heaven. These are pancakes as God intended them to be.

One morning not long after we were married, Amy — God love her — whipped up some kind of gloppy wheat-grain goo, turned the griddle on low, and then immediately plopped a few amoeba-shaped blobs onto it. No butter, no sizzle, no bubbles. I'm not sure how she decided when to flip her "pancakes" (as she mistakenly called them), but they still looked awfully doughy, in my humble opinion.

Then she dumped them on a plate, poured some kind of watery liquid over them that she said was "healthy," and tried to slide them in front of me. Now, under ordinary circumstances, I'm all for healthy options, but pancakes don't qualify as "ordinary" circumstances. Do them right or don't do them at all!

As Amy returned to her lukewarm griddle to pour some more, I slid the plate away from me. She whipped around to face me, cocked one eyebrow, and frowned.

"What?" she asked.

"You're not doing it right!" I informed her.

She looked a little surprised. "Um … yes. Yes, I am."

"No, you're not!" I insisted.

The color of her face clearly communicated her frustration to me, but just to make sure I got the message, she added, "Yes. I. Am."

I moved toward her and held out my hand for her spatula. "Here, let me show you how to do it."

Her body flinched as she rotated her shoulder toward me like an NFL linebacker and jerked the spatula out of my reach. "No! I'm not moving!"

"Listen, Amy," I said, "this is important to me." And I stepped forward.

She jabbed her shoulder up and into my chest, bodychecking me backward, and snapped, "No! It's important to *me!*"

Now, of course I've become much godlier since then, but at the time, I said something that wasn't very holy, and I moved toward her again. This time she turned the spatula on me like a weapon, flinging her lethal pancake glob at me and yelling, "Get out of my kitchen!"

Because I was such a grownup and a genius, of course I yelled back, "No, you get out of my *house!*"

And that was the beginning of our learning how to fight fair.

FIXING THE DRIP

Now, how could something so insignificant cause such a stupid fight? But that same thing happens to all of us in our relationships all the time. I'll bet you probably fought over something silly recently. And if you haven't fought about anything dumb in a while, don't let that stop you — you probably still have time before you go to bed tonight!

Scripture makes it clear that couples will indeed disagree. Proverbs 27:15 says, "A quarrelsome wife is like the dripping of a leaky roof in a rainstorm." Here "quarrelsome" can mean argumentative, combative, contentious, touchy, ill-tempered, or cross. You might experience this from your wife as nagging, manipulation, or criticism. Her constant complaining is like a *drip, drip, drip, drip, drip, drip, drip, drip, drip* to your soul.

You may not be aware that there's another, much less quoted verse, about quarrelsome husbands. It says, "It is better to suffer severe hemorrhoids than to live with a husband who's a jerk" (2 Craig 4:2 New Revised Ladies' Edition). If you've never heard that verse before, that's because it's not actually in the Bible; I made it up. But it should be! There are certainly plenty of verses addressing husbands.

Here's the reality: All couples fight. Why? Well, the short answer is because we're all sinners, and our sinfulness leads us to do selfish things. It's inevitable, unavoidable, and inherent in any relationship where true intimacy occurs. All couples fight, but healthy couples fight fair. Unhealthy couples fight dirty, with below-the-belt jabs, sucker punches, angry accusations, and bitter grudges. Healthy couples fight for resolution. Unhealthy couples fight for personal victory.

Dr. John Gottman, a marriage specialist and researcher, published a fascinating study about how couples fight, drawn from data he compiled over sixteen years. Dr. Gottman claimed he could observe a couple arguing for just five minutes and determine with ninety-one percent accuracy whether that couple would remain together or divorce. His research makes a compelling argument that relationship success is based not on *whether* you fight (because all couples do fight) but on *how* you fight. Healthy couples fight with respect for each other, with both people working toward a solution they can agree on.

If you have committed to follow Christ, then you need to fight fair in all your relationships. James says, "Everyone should be quick to listen, slow to speak and slow to become angry, because human anger does not produce the righteousness that God desires" (1:19 – 20). This inspiration from God's Spirit offers us three simple tips on how we can fight fair, not dirty.

1. QUICK TO LISTEN

When a fight is brewing, we tend to let things escalate quickly. It's not easy, but take the initiative: do your part to try to calm things down. When you feel like arguing about something your spouse just said — and you will — instead work on becoming "quick to listen."

As soon as you realize your partner is upset, you should get laser focused on what they're actually saying. Ignore the tone if you can (and the volume) and try to just listen to their words.

Honestly, this is a real challenge for me. I tend to try to keep a lot of plates spinning at once. So it's tough for me to concentrate on just one thing at a time. One day, I was texting a pastor on staff when Amy came in and said, "I need to talk to you about something important."

I thought to myself, "Craig, you need to put the phone down and listen to her." But the arrogant dude inside me immediately shot back, "That's silly, man. You know you can do two things at once!"

Unfortunately, because it takes me several times to learn from my mistakes, even as Amy started sharing some details with me — important things that I actually really needed to know — I kept right on texting.

After a few minutes, she paused. She asked, "Honey, are you even listening to me?"

Without looking up, I said, "Uh-huh. Sure."

She went on a little more, then stopped again. "Are you *really* listening?"

Still texting: "Yes. I told you I was, baby."

She continued for a while. Then she finally said, "So now I really need your feedback. Obviously, we have a few decisions we need to make here."

I finished texting and looked up. "Okay, yeah. Now, you mean about what exactly? What parts do you need decisions from me?"

Then I asked her another question, one that I wouldn't have needed to ask had I actually been listening to her.

She glared. "You have *got* to be kidding me. Seriously? You were only *half* listening. You haven't been paying attention to me this whole time. You don't value me!"

And she was right. Regardless of how I truly feel about Amy, my actions clearly demonstrated where I was placing her in my priorities in that moment. Fortunately for me, God is good, so just a few minutes later, he gave me a way out of my bind. I went back to Amy to talk to *her* about something, and this time *she* was texting. I asked her if she could talk for a minute, and without looking up, she said, "Uh-huh."

I started telling her what I needed to say, but I could tell she wasn't really "there." I asked her, "Are you listening?"

"Uh-huh."

I waited for a few seconds, and I could see she was wrapped up in what she was doing. So I said, "So, like I was saying, when I went outside to check on the kids, a giant man-eating housecat with opposable thumbs came crashing out of the woods. We all started running, but Joy just wasn't fast enough, so it got her. Sorry, honey. That one was my bad."

"Oh, it's okay," she said, without looking up.

I said, "You were only *half* listening! You haven't been paying attention to me."

She stopped and looked up at me. "I know! I'm sorry." Then she looked back down at her phone, curled her lips in a wicked little smile, and went, "Meeeeeow."

We should be quick to listen. There's a lot to be said for simplicity. Of course, you should listen to your spouse all the time. But especially when you sense that a conflict could arise, that should be your cue to stop and focus, to pay careful attention to what the other person is saying.

2. SLOW TO SPEAK

While we need to be quick to listen, before we open our mouth to respond, we also need to put on the brakes. Too often couples who fight dirty instead of fighting fair do just the opposite. They're slow to listen and quick to mouth off. Maybe you've heard this old saying: "When you're working your mouth, your ears stop working." Proverbs 18:2 says something similar: "Fools find no pleasure in understanding but delight in airing their own opinions." In other words, a fool says, "Hey, I don't really care what *you're* saying, but let me tell you what *I'm* thinking."

This happens to a lot of us during arguments. We have some important thought, some position we think crucial for the other person to understand. And usually, as soon as our focus comes back to us, we stop listening, waiting for them to take a breath so we can interrupt. If we stop listening, we can't understand their position. We want to be heard, to get to make our point. We want to "win." Scripture says that's foolish. And it's not fighting fair.

What's the best way to be "slow to speak"? Just stop talking. Or as Proverbs 21:23 puts it, "Watch your tongue and keep your mouth shut" (NLT). Isn't that a great verse? Well, maybe not to quote to your spouse in the middle of a fight. Slowing down and thinking before you speak may seem obvious, but this is one of the hardest things to do. And yet it can carry extraordinary payoffs.

If you can sense that a fight is imminent, before you say *anything*, get control and zip your lip. Then ask yourself these two questions:

1. Should what I'm thinking be said?
2. Should what I'm thinking be said *right now?*

Let's say you're about to head out the door on your way to the airport, and your spouse says, "Oh! I want to rinse these dishes before we go."

Now, that might cause you to think, "Why would you want to do the dishes right now? That's going to make us late for the airport!"

Instead, ask yourself, "Should what I'm thinking be said?"

It may not be something that needs to be said at all. Are you *really* running that late? If you work together and rinse the dishes quickly, can you realistically still get to where you're going on time? If you can, just think how much goodwill that could buy you with your spouse. But if not, ask yourself, "Should what I'm thinking be said *right now?*"

Then think very carefully how you can most lovingly communicate what you want to say. Because once those words are out there, you can never take them back. Avoid the temptation to say something like, "Why do you want to do the dishes? So in case a burglar breaks in while we're gone, he won't see our dirty dishes?"

And for sure don't say something like, "Are you some kind of psycho?"

(Not that I would ever do this. Except maybe only once. But I learned my lesson, so I'll never do that again.)

Even if you have legitimate issues, things that you really do need to address so you can work through them together, the middle of a fight is absolutely not the right place to do that. Instead, stay focused on the issue at hand. Keep your fighting fair and on topic, and work toward resolution on just that one issue.

3. SLOW TO ANGER

Obviously, when we're quick to listen and slow to speak, it makes it easier to slow down the anger. Emotions are already involved from the moment an argument begins. Your feelings can get hurt easily. But if you start to feel angry, try to see that as a great opportunity.

You're probably thinking, "What did he just say?"

Here's what I mean: Those emotions are telling you exactly where the heat is. If you can catch yourself long enough to ask, "Why does this one thing seem to bother me *so much?*" that's huge! It's like a big neon arrow pointing out a soft spot in your relationship, an area where you need the Holy Spirit to get involved. If you can see it as the gift it is, then you can start working toward resolution. And that can bring tremendous healing to your marriage long-term.

Even when you don't agree with the other person, you can still validate their feelings. That's so important, I'm going to say it again: even when you don't agree with the other person, you can still validate their feelings. Let's say your spouse says something to you like, "Sometimes, when you do [blank], it makes me feel [blank]."

You may not even understand *why* what you did made them feel that way, but that doesn't make their feelings any less valid. Feelings are real. We all have them. There's no sense getting upset with someone because they have feelings. They can't help it any more than you can. So instead, if you're actually listening — which, remember, you're supposed to be — then take a moment to validate what they've just told you they're feeling. Repeat to them what they've said to let them know you heard them and acknowledge their feelings. Try saying something like, "What I hear you saying is that when I do [blank], that makes you feel [blank]."

You'd be amazed how such a simple statement can defuse an emotional time bomb. You don't even have to agree. You just need to acknowledge that you're listening and that you're *trying* to understand. That goes such a long way.

"When I left my socks on the floor, that made you feel like I didn't value your housecleaning."

"When I didn't call to let you know I was running late, that made you feel like I didn't care about your time."

One of the best ways you and your spouse can become slow to anger is by communicating regularly and honestly when you're not facing conflict. As someone who's been married to the same person for more than two decades, I know how incredibly significant this habit can be. In fact, this may be the most practical tip I can give you: Work on your marriage during non-conflict times. Amy and I call these "marriage checkups." This relationship checkup involves three simple parts:

1. Carve Out Some Time

Plan an evening when you can get all the kids fed, bathed, and in bed at a decent time, maybe even just a little earlier than usual. This doesn't have to be a lot of time; even an hour can give you plenty of time to have a good conversation. When everybody has their favorite stuffed animal, they've had a story and a drink of water and a prayer, and they've all been snuggled, you two get alone together.

Close the door and give yourselves some privacy. It doesn't have to be a deep conversation, and it doesn't have to lead to sex.

(But it's okay if it does!) It's simply about listening and focusing on the other person without all the usual distractions.

2. Express Gratitude for Your Spouse

Take a few minutes to answer for each other, "What are three things I do that bless you?" As each of you is giving your answers, you're creating positive momentum for your time together. You're also giving your spouse the opportunity to communicate to you the things you do that make a difference to them. What I mean by this is that sometimes I may do things for Amy that *I* think are helpful, when what she actually needs may be something else.

For example, she told me once that one of the most romantic things I can do for her is to get all the kids through their bath and bedtime routines myself, buying her a little quiet time to herself before bed. Amy is crazy about our kids, and she cherishes every moment she has with them, so I probably wouldn't have guessed that was something she'd appreciate my doing for her. But now that I know she does, it actually makes *me* happy when I get to do it for her.

3. Offer Practical Feedback

Now take a few minutes and answer for each other, "What are three things I could do to be an even bigger blessing to you?" Because you've started positive, and because you've set this time aside as a safe, loving place, you can address those issues that could make your marriage better. You genuinely want to live happily together for your whole lives. That means both of you are going to have to compromise occasionally. This is a great time to process useful feedback from your lover, like, "Well, to be honest, when you [blank], it makes me feel [blank]."

Or it may be, "When you *don't* [blank], it makes me feel [blank]."

The comfortable environment you've set up has now provided you with some really great information, and in the best possible way you could get it. Because you're both in a good place, you can honestly think about what your spouse has said, and think through practical ways you can best demonstrate your love for your spouse going forward.

FIGHT CLUB

Even if you do everything else that I've suggested up to this point, it's inevitable: you're still going to fight sometimes. How do I know? Because everybody fights. Just remember: unhealthy couples fight dirty, to win; healthy couples fight clean, toward resolution. If you're already married, I'd like to give you some ideas for ground rules you can use to keep your fights clean. And even if you're not married, whether you're dating, engaged, or hopeful, the best time to think about and sort out rules for fighting is before you need them.

When Amy and I became engaged, we invested some time together to establish rules for our relationship. We wanted to set a higher standard for our marriage, so we turned to the Bible for wisdom. We memorized several verses, and we agreed on what we wanted our Groeschel family values to be. (Obviously, these are *our* rules. You should work together to define your own rules, based on what's most important to the two of you as a couple.)

1. *Never call names.* Unless, of course, it's a genuinely lovey pet name, like, say, Schmoopsie Poo or Captain Sexy. And even if you have pet names, allow them to be used only in love. Never pollute your special nicknames with sarcasm in the heat of an argument.

2. *Never raise your voice.* Nothing good can come of that. If you even begin to sense your voice is starting to rise, take a timeout. Count to ten, take a few deep breaths, sing a song, say a prayer (or fourteen). Do whatever you have to do, whatever it takes, to get yourself calmed down.

3. *Never get historical.* That's not a typo. I didn't mean "hysterical." I mean this: "You know, even back when

we were dating fifteen years ago, you ..." Don't do that. Love keeps no record of wrongs (1 Cor. 13:5). Scorecards have no place in your relationship.

4. *Never use words like "never" or "always."* If you say, "You *never* put your socks away!" that's *always* an exaggeration. If they've put their socks away even just one time, then using a word like *never* means you're not being truthful. Stick to truth: "I *feel* like *a lot of the time* you [blank], and that makes me *feel* [blank]." That's honest, and it communicates your feelings without being accusatory. Or extreme.

5. *Never threaten divorce.* If you've truly committed to "never give up," then threatening divorce is a manipulation tactic you're using just to try to win this particular argument. Or you're just being cruel. Either way, nothing good is going to come from a threat. And especially not this thermonuclear option. Don't do it.

6. *Never quote your pastor during a fight.* Leave us preachers out of it. "Pastor Craig said ...!" No, you got yourself into this; you need to get yourself out of it. Your issues are your issues. I wasn't even there when this started. (I was probably at home making pancakes!) So just leave me out of it.

ANGER MANAGEMENT

Even though we should be "slow to anger," this doesn't mean anger won't come. If you think about it, it actually means just the opposite: you *will* get angry, so take your time getting there. This means managing your anger in a way that would be pleasing to God, allowing him to lead you.

Sometimes, there are just some things you have to learn to let go of. If you want to have a great marriage, you have to be able to look at certain situations from a purely practical perspective and say, "You know what? This just isn't worth fighting over."

When Amy has the opportunity to counsel with women, a lot of the time she tells them, "Listen, you married a *man*, right? Men do *men* things, and women do *women* things. Every difference between you doesn't have to turn into some big 'issue.' You *want* your husband to be different from you! If you're both the same, one of you is unnecessary. So sometimes, you just have to let some things go."

Believe me, I know it can be hard to be slow to get angry. But let's look at another bit of biblical wisdom on marriage: " 'In your anger do not sin': Do not let the sun go down while you are still angry, and do not give the devil a foothold" (Eph. 4:26 – 27).

Did you realize that it's not a sin to get angry? Notice that this verse also assumes that we will get angry sometimes. In fact, it's actually okay to get angry sometimes. It's perfectly normal (as long as that's not your default mode). Then why would this verse even mention sin at all? Because your anger can *lead* you to sin. It all depends on what you do with your anger.

One thing you shouldn't do with it is put it to bed. If you're mad, don't go to sleep. Don't get in bed and pretend to go to sleep if you and your spouse still have unresolved issues. Legendary comedienne Phyllis Diller used to say, "Never go to bed mad. Stay up and fight." And she's right! Talk to each other. Get things out in the open. Don't do it to win. Do it to get resolution between you.

Finally, consider the last part of this verse: "Do not give the devil a foothold." What is *that* supposed to mean? Maybe you think that sounds like an exaggeration. But I've talked to so many couples over the years who just constantly left issues unresolved between them. In many of their stories, they even felt it had gotten serious enough they were considering ending the marriage. And they didn't arrive there after just one disagreement.

In every single case, they let their anger go one day. Then the next day when they woke up, that rift was just a little wider. They still didn't address it, and the next day, they had drifted even farther apart. They continued ignoring their unresolved issues day after day. And what had started one day, years ago, as a pretty simple issue had compounded until it became needlessly complex. By not resolving it early, they left the door to their marriage cracked open and the devil stuck his foot in it. Don't allow your unresolved anger to open the door to bigger problems.

TOE THE LINE

Don't go to bed angry. Work it out. One reason I'm passionate about this is because we didn't always stay up to work things out. Earlier in our marriage, we'd end a day without finishing a fight. Instead of staying up and working things out, we'd go through the motions of going to sleep as if we weren't really boiling inside.

In this mindset, we'd go to bed like gladiators and assume our fighting positions: back-to-back, with her facing one wall and me facing the other. In most marriages, one fighter suffers in silence. The other is what I call the huffer. In our marriage, Amy's the silent one. She can just lie there, not moving, not breathing. She doesn't want to give me the satisfaction of knowing she's even still alive.

I'm the huffer. I can hold out for maybe five minutes without making any noise, but we both know it's inevitable. At some point, I'm going to start flopping around, tugging at the covers, grunting and snorting. Eventually, I'll have to get up to go to the bathroom (because that's what happens at night when you're a man in your midforties). But before I come back to bed, I have to make sure I slam the toilet lid back down nice and hard. (It just wouldn't be right for me to let her get a wink of sleep while I'm still mad.) Then it's right back to huffing, puffing, and tugging blankets.

When fighting dirty like this, you also make sure you don't let any body parts touch. You can never let your foot drift over into enemy territory because you might accidentally brush. If the other person brushes your toe, you're obligated to pull away immediately. "You're not getting any toe from me tonight. You know what? You want some toe? Go play with your own toe!"

The problem, of course, is that in our anger, we're not supposed to sin. Our anger isn't going to help us accomplish the righteous life that God desires. But you know the simplest thing you can do to help you avoid getting this far gone? We actually discussed it in the last chapter, remember? *Pray together.*

Yes, it really is that simple. Seek God together in prayer. Praying together is flossing, a simple discipline you need to do every day to keep your relationship healthy. And if you miss a day, get right back to it today. Stick with it. Praying together helps you fight fair.

Here's how this works: If you're continually seeking God together every day, guess what happens when a fight starts to break out? It pops into your head that you're going to be praying together later. It's hard to both fight and pray with somebody. It's hard to throw your high-heeled shoes at somebody and then pray with them later. It's hard to say something mean and hurtful to your wife and then go before God a few hours later and ask him to make you into the man he wants you to be. It's hard to be intimate with God and live in ongoing bitterness and unforgiveness.

Once you get in the habit of seeking God and trying to hear from his Spirit, that spills over into other parts of your life. Then when you feel your emotions getting the better of you, those old tensions starting to rise again, you're able to catch yourself before you start reacting with that old sinful flesh, hitting below the belt, fighting dirty. Instead of reacting in the flesh, you learn to *respond* by the Spirit.

HELP WANTED

As I'm writing this, I'm well aware there's no way I can know the specifics of what every couple will face. You might be fighting because you don't like the way your husband chews his food when you're out in public. Or you are fighting because it frustrates you that your wife leaves trash in the car.

Then there are those relationships at the opposite end of the spectrum. You came home from grocery shopping and caught your husband looking at porn on the internet. Or maybe you just found out your wife has been cheating on you for months with one of your closest friends. There may even be violence and abuse in your relationship.

I get it. Relationships are messy. There's a range of things that people have to deal with in their lives, and certainly one book isn't going to have all the answers for everyone. But at the same time, I'm convinced that if the two of you can find some way to seek God together, and if you'll commit to fight fair, then I believe that the presence of God can bring healing to any relationship. Having said that, you might also need to admit that what's going on is not something you can handle on your own. You might need help from outside, either from a trusted mature couple or even from a Christian marriage counselor. It's more than okay to ask for help. It's wise. With this in mind, I want to share four warning signs taken from what John Gottman calls the Four Horsemen of the Apocalypse. If you see this consistently in your marriage, you are not fighting fair and might need some help.

1. *Criticizing.* People often confuse criticizing with complaining, but they're not the same thing. Complainers say, "I wish we could have left when I wanted to." Critics say, "You always make us late!" Complaining is expressing unhappiness with circumstances. Criticizing is expressing disapproval of someone's character or decisions. Complaining

is general and may not be about anyone in particular. Criticizing is specific, and it *absolutely* is about someone. If criticism is a common element in your relationship, you're headed for trouble, and you need to get some help. Criticism unchecked will carry you straight to the next warning sign.

2. *Contempt*. Contempt means despising. You don't respect or value your spouse's opinion or perhaps even your *spouse*. You somehow feel your spouse "doesn't deserve" you, or you've decided they're "not good enough" for you. Contempt often manifests in visible or audible ways. When you say something, your spouse groans or rolls their eyes. They may speak to you with sarcasm and disdain. Contempt often begins in private interactions, where it's just the two of you, as your spouse tries to keep up appearances for outsiders. But once contempt has put down roots, others outside the relationship will soon be able to see its branches blossoming with poisonous buds.

3. *Defensiveness*. Defensiveness is one of the most common warning signs that you need outside help. At least one spouse (and often both) refuses to accept any responsibility for the challenges facing the relation-

ship. People who are defensive say things like, "It's her fault. I didn't do anything wrong. She's just mad all the time." Or, "He's a jerk. His spiritual gift is 'being an idiot.'"

They may not be this blatant in their blame-shifting, but their own personal teflon coating makes sure nothing sticks to them. The problem with not accepting responsibility is, of course, that you're *both* involved. Even if one of you *is* actually undermining the relationship, then responding with God's Spirit, rather than reacting with your emotions, is the only appropriate response. Simply blaming everything on the other person is never going to move you toward resolution.

4. *Stonewalling.* Stonewalling is a passive-aggressive method used by immature people to force getting their way. A person who stonewalls either may have already given up on the relationship entirely or they're hoping they can just hold on until the present crisis "blows over." Either way, this is another angle on refusing to accept responsibility. Whether it's always changing the subject when an issue comes up, dodging discussions (sometimes by walking away or hiding), or refusing to acknowledge that a problem

even exists, stonewalling represents pretty much the opposite of pursuing restoration.

One of the most important pillars you need so you can have the relationship God wants for you is fighting fair. But even if you see one of these four things happening in your marriage — or all of them — that doesn't mean it's too late! God can heal your marriage. It's just that it's up to you to take that first step. For your part, start seeking him immediately. Don't wait. Even if you don't think your spouse is willing to seek God together with you right now, don't let that stop *you!*

If you think there's no way your marriage will work, I'd like to remind you of something Jesus said once: "With man this is impossible, but with God all things are possible" (Matt. 19:26). So where is all this tension coming from? Well, another thing Jesus said is that "the thief comes only to steal and kill and destroy." But Jesus came so that you could "have life, and have it to the full" (John 10:10).

You have only one enemy, and it's not your spouse. Get focused on that. Your enemy is a thief who's trying to steal your joy, kill your love, and destroy your marriage. The good news is you don't have to fight fair with that guy. No, with him, you're actually going to fight to win. You're going to fight for your marriage, and you're going to fight for victory.

One of the very best ways you can do that is to learn to fight fair with your spouse — for resolution, for restoration. Whatever it takes, work through everything, even the hard things. Practice forgiveness. Sacrifice your pride for love. Open up to each other and learn how to graciously give and take. Seek God together, putting him first in your relationship.

Don't fight each other.

Fight for the marriage you both long to have.

AMY'S ANGLE

When I look back on some of the things Craig and I fought about when we first got married, more than twenty-three years ago now, I'm pretty embarrassed at how silly I was. So many of those things seem ridiculous now. Of course, they didn't seem petty or silly at the time. Everything, every "issue," really felt ... well, serious.

Craig already told you about how he had to have his pancakes just so, perfectly shaped, so thin they were almost crispy, chock-full of processed ingredients, and too hot even to eat. I like pancakes too, but I like mine much thicker and made from whole wheat. God forbid that either one of us should compromise! (Although in recent years, he's learned to appreciate my healthy version, and I occasionally spoil him with those unhealthy, thin pancakes he loves so much.) There were plenty of other seriously petty arguments as well as real times of disappointed expectations and wounded feelings to work through.

When we drive somewhere new, I am always happy to have our time alone together in the car.

Typically, Craig drives, and I handle directions and navigate for him. But honestly, I don't always care whether we are on time to wherever we are going. It is much more important to me to kind of just keep things laid back and enjoy the trip. I like taking in the scenery out the window and try to relish each moment. (Important news flash: our personalities are so different!) Craig teases me that I try to steer him by the sun and the stars, which just drives him crazy. Especially if he makes a wrong turn. And if I feel like he is making us rush unnecessarily, and if I tell him so, things can get heated pretty quickly. You get the picture?

There are two things that I think have really helped us fight more fairly now. I would say both of them are tied to how much we've matured over the years in our relationship, not just with each other but with Christ. The first is that we both really know how to love each other better. Like I said, we're different— very different. But instead of letting that be a source of tension between us, we've learned not just to accommodate our differences but actually to cherish them.

I no longer try to change Craig to become more like me. Why would I want to have to deal with another me anyway? Craig is Craig. I accept him for him. Jesus does, so why shouldn't I? We don't just make allowances for each other's weaknesses or differences; we've learned to be strong for each other. We're better as a team than either one of us could ever be on our own. Our blended uniqueness creates a sweet harmony when we choose grace over pride. Just as God's Word describes marriage, we really are two halves of one person.

The second thing is that we've learned to use self-control by holding back our first thoughts during critical moments. If you're upset, it's so easy to just let those angry words fly. God really changed this in Craig's life first, and then his godly example led me to a better place too. If you can patiently and prayerfully hold back until your head clears and your heart calms, the passion of that moment just kind of dissipates. It's amazing how much easier it is to talk things through if you can just wait until a little later.

We both always know that, inevitably, before we go to sleep that same night, we're going to work things out. Then the next day, everything seems better, and we can start fresh and in love, determined not to allow any baggage to accumulate. We don't give our problems even the slightest chance to grow.

When the devil tries to stick his foot in that door, we just relentlessly keep slamming it on him until he has no choice but to back off.

Of course, that works only if you both keep on the same page. The two critical things you have to remember are constantly to seek God together through prayer and always to keep resolution as your ultimate goal. So many times when we find ourselves in an argument, we let our emotions get tangled, and they make everything messy. It's probably our pride most of all. We can get so stuck on having to be right. Besides being a terrible objective to have in a fight, it actually makes that fight unwinnable. If you win every fight, but you destroy your relationship in the process, what have you really won? Nothing!

So don't fight to win. You both should fight to lose the conflict and gain a closer relationship. Don't fight each other; fight together to see the relationship restored. Redefine winning to mean that at the end of every fight, you're closer to each other than you were when you started. That's winning! And that's what it really means to fight fair.

HAVE FUN

Let the wife make the husband glad to come home,
and let him make her sorry to see him leave.
— Martin Luther

When Amy and I were dating, I loved arranging these elaborate dates to keep things fun and unpredictable. I didn't have much money, so I usually had to get really creative. For instance, I took her on a camping date once — indoors. That's right, indoors. I borrowed my next-door neighbor's tent and set it up in my living room. A forest of houseplants and all the stuffed animals my little sister could spare surrounded the tent like wild animals peering out of the woods.

When Amy came over, I "cooked out" and served up camp-fire grub. You may be rolling your eyes and thinking that's the corniest thing you've ever heard, but she loved it. She was thrilled that I had gone to so much trouble for her. We laughed and giggled through the whole date, just being silly and enjoying each other's company.

And you know what? More than twenty-three years and six kids later, it worked! (And I am so thankful it did.) Other dates were just as fun and adventurous. We especially loved going on picnics, sometimes spontaneously. We'd just pack a few things and go someplace really beautiful (a park) or fun (the zoo), or both. We'd chat and learn about each other, sharing stories and revealing more about our lives, laughing and joking a lot.

Sometimes I'd bring her little trinkets and presents. On one of our dates, I gave her a children's book called *Miffy's Bicycle*, about a little rabbit who dreamed of getting her first bike. When I handed it to her, she said, "What's this for?"

I said, "Well, I found this book and I thought, 'Aw, this is so cute! I'd love to read it to my kids someday.' So I wanted you to keep it in a special place until we get to read it to our children."

I know, I know. Women who just read that paragraph went, "Aww!" Men who read it were like, "Dude. Seriously?" But it's true! I actually did that. And every one of my kids had every page of that book memorized by the time they were too old for it anymore. And every one of them knows, "Daddy gave this book to Mommy before I was even born." It will be a treasured keepsake in our family, hopefully for generations. In fact, years from now, when Amy and I are gone, our kids will probably have to have a dramatic legal battle to decide who gets it. (Not really. We included a paragraph about it in our will.)

You likely have your own silly, funny-to-no-one-else, special, sentimental stories. (And if you don't, then you're overdue to make some!) But having fun together is not just a big part of your dating history. Having fun in your marriage should be an ongoing series of current events.

LOVIN' YOU IS FUN

When Amy and I were dating, we devoted a lot of energy to making sure we had fun together. And when we wed, we committed to carry that same intentionality to have fun into our marriage. We knew, without even having to think about it, that having fun was really important to our relationship. We had already seen enough of our friends start losing touch with each other shortly after they got married. They fell into all those expected "grownup" married roles, and most seemed to lose sight of how much they simply enjoyed being together.

Why does that happen? While both partners are responsible for keeping the fun alive, I believe the problem often begins with the man. We're wired to be pursuers, initiators, hunters.

We're exhilarated by the chase. We love to win, to conquer, to make the kill. And guys, what do we do when we make the kill, when we get that deer? We have the head stuffed, we mount it on the wall, we brag about it for a while, and then what? We want to go hunt the next thing.

A lot of guys don't seem to be able to separate that wiring from their dating lives. You feel like you have an audience cheering you on when you're trying to get *that* girl to go out with you. You convince her to be your girlfriend. Then you try to impress her that you're good husband material, bringing her flowers and playing with other people's kids. Finally, one day you get to slip that ring onto her finger, and all your friends and family are like, "Yay! He did it! She's fantastic! Way to go, buddy!"

Then once all the cheers have died down and your quiet, everyday life begins, that crowd just vanishes. Nobody's encouraging you anymore with, "You can do it! Go get her, man!" If you don't adjust your game to your new reality, you'll lose track of the fun.

Unfortunately, too many people see fun in marriage as a luxury. "We don't have time for fun anymore. We don't have money for silly dates or weekends away. We're too busy trying to make a living and get ahead. We have to be grownups now. Sure, that was fun while it lasted, but that's all over now. I wish we still had fun, but that's not really realistic at this point in our lives." If and when the couple begins expanding their family with kids, then it begins to feel impossible for just the two of them to have fun.

But that's so not true! Let me tell you something: when you're married, fun is not a luxury; it's a requirement. I don't know why more people don't seem to be having fun in their marriages, but it's a problem I notice often. In fact, I heard one guy say, "A man doesn't know what happiness is until he gets married. But then it's too late to do anything about it!" Then not long after that, I heard a woman shoot back, "Whenever I hear a man say his wife can't take a joke, I try to remind him that she already took the biggest one when she married him."

I know so many couples who used to have a blast when they were dating, but then once they got married, "life" intruded, and over time, they just kind of stopped enjoying each other.

Without romance, without adventure, without physical intimacy — without *fun* — marriage is reduced to a simple business arrangement. You're like partners in a company, two roommates who split expenses like rent and food, yet living entirely different lives. Your communication can end up like short meetings in which you're divvying up to-do lists:

"I'll take Jamie to her gymnastics practice on Thursday."

"Okay. Her meet this week is at the same time as Beth's piano lesson, so I'll take Beth to that while you guys are there. Did you pay the Visa bill?"

"Yeah, but somehow I managed to forget to take the utility payment with me, so we still need to get that in the mail."

"Well, I have to go by the ATM this morning anyway. There's a mailbox right by there. Just give it to me and I'll drop it off."

"Thanks. Now, what's the next item on this week's agenda?"

Don't get me wrong. All of these are important responsibilities that have to get taken care of. But if you let your relationship deteriorate to the point that everything is about simply negotiating the day's transactions, then you'd better get as much enjoyment as you can licking those stamps for the bills, if you know what I mean.

People never fall in love having a bad time. Have you ever known someone who fell in love with a person they were bored with? Have you ever heard a young woman say, "Oh, this guy is just awesome! We soooo have nothing in common. Every time we get together, we just sit there and don't say anything. Sometimes I'll even sit and watch him veg out playing video games for hours. It's such a turn-on when he's all dull and boring like that."

No! You hear things like, "We have so much fun when we get together! It's crazy how much we have in common. The hours slip by like minutes. The worst part of every date is when we have to say goodbye. It seems like we never have enough time to talk about all the things we really want to. I wish we could just be together forever."

If people didn't have fun dating, there's no way they'd get married. But doesn't it seem like some couples, after they get married, just lose their sense of adventure and fun?

Don't think you have time to have fun? On the contrary, you don't have time *not* to have fun. In fact, if you don't have some fun in your marriage, one day you may not have a marriage.

HEADLINES AND DETAILS

God wants us to have fun with our spouses. He genuinely takes delight in seeing us enjoy the blessings of marriage. Marriage gives color to what often feels like a black-and-white kind of life. "Live happily with the woman you love through all the meaningless days of life that God has given you under the sun. The wife God gives you is your reward for all your earthly toil" (Ecc. 9:9 NLT). The New International Version of this verse encourages us to "Enjoy life with your wife, whom you love." It doesn't get much simpler than that, does it?

There are a lot of days that you just have to go about your business, getting things done. You get up, go to work, maybe take a break for lunch, work some more, then finally come home at the end of the day. And that's the best part of every day: getting back to the woman you love. Guys, be intentional about pursuing happiness together with her because she's God's "reward" in your life.

Coming home to your spouse means enjoying face-to-face time. This means just what you'd expect: spending time together, in person, enjoying each other's company. When you're dating, it seems like you can just talk and talk and talk for hours on end every day. You call each other on the phone and talk. Then between calls you're texting back and forth. I've known couples who were dating who would talk to each other on the phone until two in the morning. Then, when they finally ran out of things to say, they'd lay their phones next to them on the pillow and fall asleep listening to each other breathe. (I'm not talking about heavy breathing here, just a normal, appropriate breathing rate!)

Then what happens when we get married? For most people, all of that face-to-face time fills up with schedules and responsibilities and stress: which person is picking up the kids after school, "you've got to get him to karate," "you've got to get her to dance," "we need to get the oil changed in the van," "swing by and pick up some milk on your way home," "I think the air conditioner may be going out," and "okay, I'll call the guy to come have a look." Even though you're face to face, even though you're spending time together, you're using it all up simply exchanging information, not communicating, not sharing your below-the-surface selves. It may be civil, but it's not intimate. It may be practical, but it's certainly not fun. And worst of all, it's not working. Both of you need legitimate face-to-face fun.

Let's look in Scripture at an example of the kind of communication I'm talking about. In Song of Solomon, Solomon poetically speaks to his beloved, the Shulammite woman, taking the time to describe every aspect of her beauty to her in intimate, saucy detail. He starts with her feet, working his way gradually up her entire body, until finally he ends up at her eyes. Please allow me to translate a portion (7:1 – 4) for you:

"How beautiful your sandaled feet, O prince's daughter! Your graceful legs are like jewels, the work of an artist's hands."

Oh, this guy is good. I like to imagine he's put on some Barry White for background music.

"Your navel is a rounded goblet that never lacks blended wine."

Translation: "Baby, I'd love to drink body shots from your belly button."

"Your waist is a mound of wheat encircled by lilies."

Translation: "You have a really pleasant hourglass shape. You look pretty and delicate. And you smell good."

"Your breasts are like two fawns, like twin fawns of a gazelle."

Translation: "I love your twins. They look so soft and fluffy and beautiful! And I can't tell you how happy I am that you have two of them." (For the record, I could definitely go into way more detail on this one, but because I'm maturing, I'll exercise restraint. But I'm sure you get the idea.)

"Your neck is like an ivory tower."

Translation: "Your neck is so long and slender. Your skin looks like porcelain."

"Your eyes are the pools of Heshbon by the gate of Bath Rabbim."

Translation: "Your eyes are soooo blue. I could just drown in those eyes, baby."

Now, what is Solomon doing here? He's talking intimately to his lady, face to face, giving her details.

Men like headlines.

Women like details.

Solomon can't help himself. And his woman loves the attention. Women enjoy talking with their husbands. They love it when we tell them what we're feeling and how we're feeling and why we're feeling it. Sure, guys just want to *show* them, but the ladies like us to put those things into words. Articulating our feelings requires us to lower our guard, which makes the relationship more real. Intimate, ongoing conversation is key to success in any marriage. That means you have to protect it, because if you don't, mark my words, everyday life will gradually elbow out that closeness, and you'll lose your face-to-face fun.

SAVE THE DATE

People who are a part of our church family probably got tired a long time ago of hearing me say the same two words over and over, every time I talk about marriage: date night. Date night, date night, date night, date night, date night. I feel like I just can't emphasize it enough. For years, almost every week, Amy and I faithfully kept to our date night. This commitment was the time we set aside every week to connect intimately and emotionally, face to face. No matter what other craziness was going on in our lives, both of us always knew we had at least one evening coming during the week that we could both look forward to.

But as we got older, and as it seemed like we were adding one kid after another, and as the church's moving parts were growing ever more complicated, eventually we caved. We talked through our schedules together and agreed, "Hey, you know what? We already have a great marriage. We're just too busy during this season of our lives to keep face-to-face date night as a sacred cow. So for now, let's just relax and have some fun with our kids."

It made perfect sense at the time. We simply had no idea how much that seemingly innocent decision would cost us. Months later, we noticed a disturbing trend in our relationship. Every week, we would get together with our small group of friends to discuss our faith and to share what was going on with us, both good and bad. During those weekly meetings, I kept noticing the same thing happening again and again. Amy would bring up something she was going through, something she was feeling, and I would think, "I didn't know she was dealing with that!"

More than just being my wife, Amy is the best friend I've ever had. And here she was bringing up really important things that I had no idea were even going on with her. Amy was noticing the same thing. I'd tell our group, "Here's what I've really been praying about recently..." or, "This is a burden I'm feeling really heavy about right now." Back at home, Amy would ask me about it. "When did that start? How come group tonight was the first time I heard about it?"

Fortunately, we came to the same conclusion at the same time. We both realized just how important that intimate face-to-face time had been in stabilizing and strengthening our marriage. As soon as we saw what was happening, we recommitted ourselves to our regular date night. It really *was* sacred!

You need to do that too. You have to carve out that time, recognize how sacred it is, and then jealously guard it. The quality of your marriage will tell on you. If you're regularly investing in face-to-face time, your relationship will show it. And you know what else it will show? If you're not.

Visiting in the car as you're driving your kids to their next activity doesn't count. Neither does talking while you're watching some TV show together. And sitting across a table from each other playing with your cell phones certainly doesn't count. You need genuine face-to-face time. Consistent, guarded, and faithful. Take long walks like those cute older couples in the mall. Go sit in a coffee shop. Take a long drive. Go to a drive-in movie. Find a cheap hole-in-the-wall restaurant and become a regular. Do whatever you have to do. Just invest in regularly scheduled, authentic face-to-face fun!

SIDE WAYS

The next kind of fun is just as important as the face-to-face kind. Side-to-side fun is simply hanging out with your best friend (your spouse), enjoying some activity together that both of you like. Song of Solomon 7:11 says: "Come, my beloved, let us go to the countryside, let us spend the night in the villages."

Can't you just feel the fun coming? "Hey, babe, let's go on a weekend getaway. Let's get out of the house, take the kids to your folks, and just go away and have some fun together. Maybe we can find a nice little bed and breakfast somewhere."

Ladies, don't underestimate how important side-to-side fun is to your husband. I don't want to generalize too much, but what I'm about to tell you is *generally* true. For most men, side-to-side fun means as much as face-to-face fun means to you. Hanging out with his wife and doing something fun makes a man feel valued. You spend face-to-face time together because you need to. You spend side-to-side time together because you *want* to. It's what bonds you as friends.

A friend of mine told me once, "When I'm walking by my wife's side, I always like to hold her hand. I do this for two reasons. The first is because I love her. The second is because if I let go, she goes shopping."

Amy and I had already been married for several years when we finally learned how important side-to-side time is. Ironically, when we did, it explained some feelings I had had about Amy way back when we first started dating. When she and I first started spending time together, one of my favorite things about her was that she *always* wanted to come along with me, no matter what I was doing. If I was meeting a buddy for tennis, she wanted to come. If I needed to go study at the library, she'd grab some books and come study too.

There was one time in particular that I think I'll probably always remember. We were in college, and I was going to pick her up so we could go meet some friends. On my way out the door, I grabbed a couple of baseball gloves. While we were hanging out with our friends later, Amy and I played a game of catch and visited. I specifically remember thinking at the time, "This chick has to be the best girlfriend ever. How in the world did I find a girl who would actually want to play catch with me?" A friend took a picture of us having a catch and gave it to me later. That picture meant so much to me, I had it blown up to poster size and kept it on my wall. I wanted everyone I knew to see my unbelievably perfect girlfriend who plays catch — smoking hot *and* she loves sports!

What would be the equivalent for you? You need to find

activities that you can enjoy together. Is your husband always asking you to go golfing with him? Maybe you think that sounds boring. But let me ask you something: have you ever actually driven a golf cart? It doesn't have to be boring. And besides, just think how much conversation time that would give you together.

Maybe he'd like you to go hunting with him. That's not my thing, but I know some wives who enjoy hunting. One woman just loves being outside and sitting quietly with her husband for hours. They hold hands, share coffee, and then riddle deer or turkeys or other unsuspecting animals with bullet holes. Doesn't that sound romantic?

Of course, you don't have to go to extremes to enjoy activities together. Maybe you like visiting a museum or building sand castles on the beach. Maybe you could go rock climbing together, or on a long hike. You might ride a tandem bicycle or play chess together. You can even just sit on your porch in the morning, having a cup of coffee together and watching birds. It doesn't matter, as long as it's side-to-side time. Ladies, try going into his world with him. But this works both ways. Gentlemen, you go into her world too. Make all the jokes you want about going shopping with her or to a craft fair or flea market or antiques auction, but you just might enjoy yourself. Both of you: take time to do something with your spouse that they enjoy.

Sometimes I go grocery shopping with Amy on Friday nights. Why? Because I'm such a huge fan of grocery shopping, of course! (Actually, I'd rather enjoy some nice Chinese water torture than compare canned vegetable prices.) But you know what? Amy enjoys going grocery shopping. She's good at it! And I enjoy that time alone with her. Besides, it gives me the opportunity to try to sneak some real pancake mix into the basket when she's not looking. In fact, the last time I went grocery shopping with Amy, she appreciated it so much that the next morning, she made me flat pancakes, just how I like them. That's how good God is, and that's how good my wife is.

Every once in a while, I've been known to let my godliness spiral out of control, even watching an entire TV show all about wedding dresses with her. I didn't even know such a show existed before, but yes, evidently, there's an entire series just about women choosing their wedding dresses. As I was sitting there with her in her world, she asked me, "Doesn't this make you feel close?" And I couldn't help smiling at how cute she was.

I regularly enjoy spending time with her in her world, doing things that she likes. I've been to a coed baby shower with her before. Once she even asked me if I'd go get a manicure with her. In that case, though, I felt like I had to draw a line somewhere. I just couldn't do that. It would creep me out too much to let somebody mess with my nails. Now, I know some guys who like getting manicures. And while I guess that's okay, just so we're clear, that's not why they call them "man"-icures. But I have this philosophy that every guy can have just one "chick" thing that he can be into. Mine is candles. If yours is your fingernails … well, okay. But you just get the one! If you start watching wedding dress shows by yourself with candles burning after having your nails manicured, we're going to have an intervention.

It's pretty much a given that women like for their men to open up and talk. So let me ask you, ladies, when is your man most likely to open up to you? I can tell you two specific times:

1. When he's doing something with you that he enjoys.
2. Immediately *after* he's done something with you that he enjoys.

(Wink, wink. Yes, there is a joke camouflaged in the two things above. But just because it's funny doesn't mean it's not true.)

PARK PLACE

Face-to-face fun matters. So does side-to-side fun. And when you have face-to-face and side-to-side fun, guess what that leads to? Belly-button-to-belly-button fun! And to demonstrate the meaning of this kind of physical fun, maybe we should let

Solomon and the Shulammite woman demonstrate for us. In Song of Solomon 7:10 – 12, Solomon's lover begins to respond to his come-ons:

"I belong to my beloved, and his desire is for me."

Translation: "I know you want me. Well, guess what? I'm all yours."

"Come, my beloved, let us go to the countryside, let us spend the night in the villages."

Translation: "Yes. I want to go on a weekend getaway with you. Why don't we go check out that little B&B you keep talking about?"

"Let us go early to the vineyards to see if the vines have budded, if their blossoms have opened, and if the pomegranates are in bloom."

Translation: "Once we get there, let's wander in the woods and look for some wildlife, if you know what I mean. And if spring is in the air ..."

"There I will give you my love."

Does that line really need any translation? Hello! She's telling him, "Let's go have sex in the park!" I want to be really clear here: I'm not suggesting you do that. I'm just saying that's what she said. If you go have sex in a park, you're going to get yourself arrested, unless you can find a really private place. (But you didn't hear that from me.)

So there you have it. That's belly-button-to-belly-button fun for you. It's romance. It's physical intimacy. You get it. (At least I hope you get it.)

Now, you might be thinking, "Is God okay with that kind of stuff?" Yes! Yes, he is. Let's look at his Word: "May your fountain be blessed, and may you rejoice in the wife of your youth. A loving doe, a graceful deer — may her breasts satisfy you always, may you ever be intoxicated with her love" (Prov. 5:18 – 19).

Translation: "Enjoy each other always. Whether you've been married for ten minutes or for forty years, enjoy the woman you married."

Isn't God's Word good? She's beautiful, she's graceful, and may you always be satisfied with what you have in her. The Hebrew word translated as "intoxicated" here is *shagah* (shah-GAH). This word is sometimes used to describe how one animal pursues, attacks, and kills another animal for food. That's how Solomon says you should feel about her love for you — that it runs you down, pounces on you, and devours you. Talk about steamy! In marriage, it's not just okay to be consumed by passion for your beloved; it's a blessing from God.

Let me share with you how you can apply Solomon's wisdom in your own marriage. Besides being an indicator of the overall health of your marriage, physical intimacy (and fun) is one of the most powerful things you can do to bring healing to your relationship. Maybe it's been awhile, or it feels like you're on different schedules. Maybe it feels like you're out of practice, or that what you've been doing hasn't been working lately. Or perhaps it's simply been boring and predictable. Don't despair; there's hope.

Let's start with the men. Guys, remember that your approach matters — a lot! Even though it may require a little extra effort, try to be creative in the ways you approach your wife. If you're always coming on to her in the same ways, say, pointing down and saying, "Hey, baby! You want some of this, don't you? You know you do!" then probably it's time to change it up. If you think it's a turn-on for her for you to slap your own butt every time you step out of the shower, "Hey! Check out *this* action!" then let's just be honest: you need to add some new tools to your toolbox.

For instance, tenderness might not matter much to you, but it might matter a great deal to your wife. What about being subtle? There's nothing seductive about aggressive nudity. Work on your approach. Try romance. Try some meaningful conversation. Bring her a gift. Send her flowers for no reason, not just to apologize for an argument. Work on your approach. Ask her about her day. Then actually listen to what she says! When she sits down, pick up one of her feet and start massaging it. Work on your approach. Is my message getting through, guys? (I hope so. Because I'm also talking to myself.)

Finally, don't always try to make everything sexual. If she

says, "We need to get the oil changed," control your urge to respond with something like, "I'll change *your* oil!"

Instead try to show her that you love her just as much whether or not you wind up making love. Maybe give her a back rub that *doesn't* end up being sexual. Try being loving instead. Try being tender. Work on your approach.

Of course, I have some advice for the ladies too: make an approach. That's it. Any approach! Just make an approach. (I hope you know I'm smiling as I write this.)

Most women would probably say they'd like to experience a little more romance in their marriage. Like Amy says (see her input at the end of this chapter), what's stopping you? Try a little romance! "Do to others whatever you would like them to do to you" (Matt. 7:12 NLT).

Ladies, whatever you've got, I can promise you it looks better in silk than it does in flannel. So throw out that ratty old bathrobe you've been wearing as a uniform. Go get yourself some nice lingerie. There are lots of comfortable options now (or so I've been told). Get a babysitter and go on a date with your husband. Draw a bath. Give a back rub. Play some music. Maybe put on some Marvin Gaye: "Let's get it on!"

Maybe you're thinking, "Well, all of that sure sounds nice, Craig. But we don't have time for that kind of stuff. We've got little kids. We can't really afford to go out right now." Then throw in a *Dora the Explorer* DVD, sneak away to your bedroom together, and lock the door. Pile a few pillows in front of the door to muffle any noise. "Quick! We've got twenty-five minutes. Go, Diego, go!"

My point is have some fun, some good old-fashioned, belly-button-to-belly-button fun. Honestly, I'd love to get a postcard from some of you nine and a half months from now announcing your beautiful new baby.

ALLIANCE OF INTIMACY

Now let's get serious for a minute here, ladies. Generally speaking, I don't think anyone would argue that most men tend to desire physical intimacy more frequently than women do. So ladies, you need to understand that when you turn off that faucet and things start to go dry, for your husband, that's a crisis. It's the equivalent of the distress you feel when there's silence, when there's no emotional intimacy between you. It's a crisis. One of the most important ways you can demonstrate love to each other is by renewing your spiritual commitment to one another through acts of physical love. Sex is spiritual. It's two people becoming one in an alliance of intimacy. It's a blessing from God, a way that you can genuinely serve one another.

Here's another thing you need to consider. If you're not meeting your husband's sexual needs, what are some likely consequences? You are his only legitimate option for feeling sexual fulfillment, after all. Everything else he could do is sinful. (And men, the same goes for you as well. If you're not meeting your wife's needs for physical intimacy, then you're setting her up to consider other options.) Make no mistake: one of the greatest things you can do for each other is to engage in frequent, creative, spiritual lovemaking. It is a gift from God that honors him by renewing your spiritual covenant to one another.

Maybe you're thinking, "But he's a jerk! I really don't like him very much right now, and I don't like you for telling me I should have sex with him."

I can understand that. When someone hurts your feelings — by withdrawing, by rejecting, by criticizing — then it makes sense that you don't want to be anywhere near this person. I get that. You might be a wife married to a jerk who cares only about himself. Or maybe you're a loving husband married to a controlling and manipulative wife. Beyond the shadow of a doubt, those are serious issues I don't want to sweep past.

What I'm about to say may be extremely difficult for you to read. It may go against everything you feel. But hang in there with me. Even when you don't feel like being close to your spouse physically, you need to remember that feelings follow actions. Revelation 2:5 says, "Consider how far you have fallen! Repent and do the things you did at first." If you want what you once had, start doing what you once did. You got married because you had fun. Start having fun again. Seek God. Pursue the One with your two. Fight fair. You had fun at one time. You could have fun again. Get creative. Make it a priority.

"But I don't like it! Besides, there's a guy at work who I think can meet my emotional needs, and he looks better than my husband!"

Or maybe, "There's this girl at the gym, and she seems like she'd be a lot more fun than my wife!"

If the grass looks greener somewhere else, it's time to water your own yard. Invest in the marriage that God has given you. Enjoy life with the wife that God blessed you with. Even when it seems like the distance between here and there is just too far to go, remember, "with God all things are possible" (Matt. 19:26). From this day forward, seek him together. He'll give you what he wants you to have as you do what's right to honor him.

And honoring God in marriage should be a lot of fun.

AMY'S ANGLE

As I know Craig's already been telling you, he and I have had a lot of fun together over the years. But those fun times didn't just happen. We've had to be really intentional in how we spend our time together. Before we had kids, when we had time on our hands, we used to enjoy some great, drawn out games of chess—yes, seriously. And of course, we'd spend most of that time talking. Now, whether it's something as simple as taking a walk together, playing tennis together, or even occasionally working out together, those opportunities we take to enjoy some time with each other often evolve into amazing, relationship-building conversations.

After twenty-odd (and I do mean odd) years of marriage (just kidding, Craig), I know our marriage is stronger than ever because we regularly prioritize our time to enjoy each other. We've always been best friends. And because we continually choose to invest in reconnecting, we expect to stay close.

Distractions are rampant. Life happens. And we've had to learn the hard way, unfortunately, how important it is to guard our time together. And when you don't, you can bet you're going to see the negative impact cropping up in your relationship. When you don't spend time together, it's those little bits of shorthand communication between the two of you that suffer. The shared concerns, the inside jokes, the way you're both attuned to the other's feelings. When you lose these, it creates distance between you, a distance that you both can feel in your hearts.

I think the most important advice I could offer to couples is simply this: prioritize your schedule. Quality time together is crucial for a thriving relationship. If you neglect each other, even for just a short season, then your relationship is likely to suffer significantly for it. For your marriage bond to grow stronger, you have to be intentional. If you find yourself in a really busy season of life, understand that it's normal. But don't settle for normal. Accept the responsibility to invest in your romance. Make a plan. Schedule it. Then stick to it.

What was it that drew you to each other in the first place? I'll bet it was fun, wasn't it? No matter how things feel now, in the beginning, you just couldn't get enough of each other. I believe the key to why that was true is that you were on a pursuit to know and be known. You have to work to keep that alive by making time for each other now, just like you did then. Creating fun moments to engage in together positively influences every other part of your marriage.

Physical intimacy is directly related to your process of growing together, and it can be a good indicator of how healthy your relationship is — or isn't. In fact, if physical intimacy has been a problem lately in your marriage, I'd be willing to bet that you've neglected being emotionally connected in other ways.

I understand that sometimes a spouse may have baggage from their past, and if that's you, I pray you'll seek healing through Christ. God can renew your mind and heart completely through his powerful, living Word. I know. He did this for me. The truth is that physical intimacy in your marriage is holy. It's a powerful way that you can both grow in Christ and a great way that you can minister love to each other. Avoiding healthy physical intimacy hurts both of you, and could allow negativity to creep into the other parts of your relationship.

So make fun times a priority in your marriage. You be the change. Aim to get back to that place where you are best friends, laughing together, snuggling, looking to each other for comfort and for joy. If you can be honest with yourself, that's what you really want anyway, isn't it? Then what's stopping you?

God wants you to have fun in your marriage!

STAY PURE

What a happy and holy fashion it is that those
who love one another should rest on the same pillow.
— Nathaniel Hawthorne

About four or five years into our marriage, I did something really stupid that hurt Amy. (I know, it's hard to believe.) I was in our bedroom watching TV, and Amy was in the adjoining bathroom doing her hair. I was sitting on our bed with the remote, just flipping through channels. (As any guy can tell you, it's never about what's on TV; it's about what *else* might be on TV.) While Amy could hear the audio of my channel surfing from where she was, she couldn't see it. She wasn't even paying attention to my cruise through the channels — or so I thought.

So I was flipping: basketball, *click*, golf, *click*, fishing show, *click*, infomercial, *click*, girls dancing in bikinis on a beach … hold on a second. And I hesitated. After lingering on that channel for several seconds, with my mind wandering a bit (not to mention my eyes), I continued on: police show, *click*, weather report, *click*, science show, *click*.

A few minutes later, Amy came out of the bathroom. She walked over to where I was sitting on the bed and sat down facing me. She didn't say anything at first. She just sat there, looking into my eyes. I stopped clicking and looked at her. We just sat there, staring at each other in awkward silence for an uncomfortably long time.

Finally, Amy broke the silence. "Why did you hesitate on that one channel?"

I could hear the hurt in her voice. My mind raced, feeding me lies I could offer to answer her. "Tell her the remote stuck! Or say, 'What? You mean on that music show? I just thought I recognized that song, so I stopped to see if I could remember what it was.'"

Of course, we both already knew the truth.

I couldn't maintain eye contact with her. I clicked the TV off and looked down at the comforter. I said weakly, "I shouldn't have. I … I'm sorry."

She reached out and put her hand under my chin, gently raising my head until our eyes met again. I could see that her eyes were wet, swollen with tears that hadn't fallen yet.

It was all I could do to maintain her gaze and not cry. I felt sick inside. Then she asked me a question I'll never forget for as long as I live. She asked quietly, "Well ... was it worth it?"

THE PRICE OF PLEASURE

"Was it worth it?" Now, you're probably thinking you know the right answer to Amy's question, both for me and for anyone else in my shoes who's facing temptation. Yet apparently there's a huge gulf between knowing the right answer and the reality of living it out.

You probably know that millions of people hope, dream, and plan to be married one day. You may be one of them right now, or you can remember when you were. They invest enormous energy into finding that one special person they want to devote themselves to loving for the rest of their lives. (Maybe that's why you're reading this book.) They spend enormous sums and devote countless hours to planning every aspect of the perfect wedding.

While every engaged couple I know plans to have a great married life together, I don't know many who plan to betray their spouse by committing adultery. Or have a raging porn addiction. Or a friend with benefits. But based on statistical evidence, not to mention all the positive reinforcement our culture provides, it has become accepted, expected even, that everyone needs to do whatever it takes to be happy. Whether it's just "a little something-something on the side" or a full-fledged affair, an emotional attachment to someone we meet online or an addiction to erotic images, everyone wants to feel good. We all want to explore our fantasies and be sexually satisfied, right? It's the twenty-first century, for heaven's sake — we're entitled to it!

Do I have your attention yet? Nobody would ever say they plan for any of these absurd, out-of-control things to happen in their lives. (At least no one we'd respect.) And yet statistics tell us that up to seventy-five percent of people get themselves entangled in at least one of these behaviors sometime after they're married. (And some people end up involved in more than just one.) How could that be? How is it that no one seems to *plan* to engage in activities that have the potential to significantly damage or even destroy their marriage (as well as their life), but then the majority of people — *most* people — still end up there?

Do you know the number-one reason dating couples cite today as the cause of breakups? Unfaithfulness. One person cheats on the other. Yet that's exactly what our society is training people to do — to be unfaithful to each other.

Most people don't seem to realize that the gap between

knowing the right thing to do and doing it is filled with quicksand. Instead of building a firm, solid bridge through a shared commitment to daily purity and fidelity to one another, a lot of people think they can find their own way across the divide. And then with each step they take, they sink a little deeper into a soggy, stinking swamp. Then one day they go under and lose their sense of direction. They forget that each little step they took toward their own pleasure was a step away from the holiness of their marriage. Each text, each flirty conversation, each website, each mouse click, each sensual fantasy.

Maybe it helps to remember that these choices aren't just poisons in your marriage but toxins in your relationship with God as well. Hebrews 13:4 is probably the best verse in the Bible that directly addresses marriage purity: "Marriage should be honored by *all*, and the *marriage bed kept pure*, for God will judge the adulterer and all the sexually immoral" (emphasis mine).

Marriage should be honored by all. What does "all" mean? Not a trick question. It means that if you're married, God expects you to honor the covenant of marriage. What it also means is that if you're *not* married, God still expects you to honor the covenant of marriage. Clearly, purity matters to God. And purity matters in your marriage, whether that's the marriage you're in right now or the marriage you hope to have one day. We can all agree on this, right?

Then let me ask you another question: Do you think adultery

is always wrong? Again, not a trick question. Most of us would probably have to agree that the answer is yes. In fact, according to a recent study, ninety percent of Americans said they feel that adultery is *always* wrong. And get this: a few decades ago, that number was actually lower than it is today. This means that in the previous generation, more people believed that adultery could potentially be acceptable in some circumstances than believe it today. Now, here's something even stranger: even though more people today claim they believe that adultery is wrong, more people today are committing adultery than in the past.

According to a study conducted by the University of California, San Francisco, in the decade between 1998 and 2008, the percentage of people committing adultery in the United States more than doubled from the previous decade. I hope that statistic alarms you as much as it does me. Clearly, we're headed in the wrong direction. Before we can address how to reverse course, I think we first need to look at why it's happening. While I'd say there are many, many reasons more people are committing adultery today than in the past, let's focus on a few areas that are within our power to control.

PRACTICING FOR DIVORCE

The first reason that more people commit adultery now is that we simply face more temptations today than people did in the past. And not only are there more ways we can get ourselves into trouble these days, the ways that we can give in are easier to take advantage of than they used to be.

I can't tell you how many times we've worked with couples in our church where one of the partners had fallen into an extramarital affair that began as just a "harmless" exchange online. Whether it seems as innocent as following someone on Twitter who shares your sense of humor, or running into an old flame on Facebook, or looking at pictures of that cute someone on Instagram, that's only the bait. What starts as a pleasant back-and-forth rarely stops there.

No, eventually you end up taking it private, with a chat or some kind of messaging. The first time, you might even feel embarrassed, deleting the evidence and vowing never to do it again. Over time, though, unless you get some help and embrace transparency, it will keep calling to you, even when you're not online, until the hook catches you. Most of these opportunities to fall into temptation didn't even exist ten years ago.

But it's not Facebook's fault. It's ours.

Facebook, Twitter, and Instagram are just three examples. There are almost innumerable ways you can get yourself into trouble online. Entire websites are devoted to helping people cheat and have affairs discreetly. You can go on Craigslist and buy a television, some used tires, or a prostitute. (Just so you know, I don't have anything to do with Craigslist. It's a completely different Craig.)

I think smartphones and tablet computers might be some of the biggest temptation game-changers. When I was a kid, if you wanted to look at pornography, you had to have a friend whose dad or big brother had a stash somewhere. Then you had to actually find it and keep secret that you knew about it.

Now you can be eleven years old with a smartphone (or have a friend who has one), and you're just a few taps away from anything you could imagine, and plenty that you wouldn't want to imagine. Not only that, you get to carry around that easy porn access twenty-four hours a day. How convenient! I believe this kind of temptation is taking people down every day, wrecking their relationships, their very lives.

Another reason I think more temptations exist today is that people are waiting longer to get married. While certainly there's nothing wrong with getting married later, when our culture has filled up with so many people waiting longer to get married, it fundamentally changes the dynamics of what it means to be "single."

This isn't rocket science. When people get married later, typically that means they're dating more people. But even if you've committed to having only pure relationships, dating more people means you're going to face more temptation, more opportunities to compromise your standards. If even the best-intentioned people give in (and statistically, most will), then dating more people means they'll end up having more sexual partners. And having more sexual partners means that when you get married, you'll be carrying more sexual baggage into that marriage.

Have you ever wondered why breakups are so painful these days? It's because people who aren't married do married things. It's actually pretty predictable. You do married things with one or two or eight or twelve or seventeen different people. Then one day, when you finally have your "real" spouse, if things get tough, what happens? You default to all that training you've been giving yourself over the years: you cut your losses and walk away. All that time with all of those "lovers," you were just practicing for divorce. And you didn't even realize it.

As we've already seen, God's standard is for everybody to keep the marriage bed pure. That's pretty straightforward. It means that "married things" are reserved for people who are married to each other. But in our culture today, even though we know it's not God's best, most couples do a lot of those married things without committing to marriage. They say things to each other like, "I love you, honey! You're the only one for me." Now of course, what they actually mean is, "You're the only one for me … right now. Technically, I guess you're my … let me see … sixteenth? No. Seventeenth 'only one.' So far. But you're my only one *today*. That's good enough, right? I love you."

We've all seen this in some of our friends' relationships, even if we choose not to do it ourselves. You know what I'm talking about. It starts with "regular" dates, but if they like each other, there's that simple, inevitable progression of what's acceptable, based primarily on physical attraction. One thing leads to another, and eventually you find yourselves trying to medal in the Couples category for Naked Gymnastics. (Don't pretend you're embarrassed. You know it's true.)

Speaking of your friends (since of course we're not talking about you), you need to learn to recognize bad advice that your friends offer you about relationships. If your friend says, "You wouldn't buy a car without taking it for a test drive first, would you?" I'd encourage you to reply with something like, "Of course not! Also, I don't know if you've noticed this, but cars and people are nothing alike. What are you, crazy?"

People are alive. Cars are not. Human beings have feelings. Minds. Souls. A car's not going to become emotionally attached to you (and you shouldn't to it). And when you ditch the car a few years from now because it's got too many miles on it, and a new model just came out that you like better, the car's feelings aren't going to be hurt. Also, you're not going to suffer remorse and guilt about how you use cars and then throw them away, constantly worrying that you're probably going to die without a car when you're old. No, there's only one place to go for a test drive — to the car dealership.

FOOD POISONING

With these contributors in mind, let's consider what we can do about them. Basically, there are two kinds of purity: inward purity and outward purity. Inward purity means what's going on in our hearts — the things we choose to think about and the things we feel. Outward purity is our behavior — the things we choose to do and choose *not* to do. Let's start outward and work in.

Paul writes, "But among you there must not be *even a hint* of sexual immorality, or of *any kind* of impurity, or of greed, because these are improper for God's holy people" (Eph. 5:3, emphasis mine). This means nobody should be able to see anything in our behavior that could give them even the slightest impression we're engaging in anything immoral or impure. Why would even just a little be too much? Because impurity is like poison; even just a little poison is too much. It takes only a little to kill your marriage. You don't want *any* amount of poison in your marriage.

Think about this. It's not like, "Oh, look ... there's a little bit of dust in my water!" No, it's like, "Hey! There's rat poison in my water!" I don't know about you, but I don't like to drink my water with rat poison. (It tastes bad, plus it can kill you.) It's not like when your mashed potatoes are touching your fried chicken. It's more like a cat suffering from diarrhea squatted on your dinner and let loose. I know that's an absolutely horrible, disgusting visual image. That's the idea! I want you to remember just how awful it is to have *any kind* of impurity in your marriage, *even a hint* of immorality.

I can't imagine anyone wanting to have anything to do with a disgusting, cat-ruined plate of food. It's like taking food poisoning to a whole new level. You should feel just as strongly about letting any hint of immorality near your relationship with your spouse.

And just so we're clear, let's take a little pop quiz on what constitutes this kind of poison for your marriage. I'll give you a scenario, and then you decide whether you think it qualifies as "a hint of sexual immorality." Answer honestly and don't get too smug — the level of difficulty increases and might hit closer to home. Ready? Let's begin.

You're married, and you have sex with someone who's not your spouse at your office. Hint of sexual immorality: yes or no?

The answer is yes.

You're married, and you have sex with your kids' babysitter. Hint of sexual immorality: yes or no?

Of course. Yes.

You're married, and you have sex with the handsome guy who cleans your pool. Just to make this one a little harder, let's say he has six-pack abs. And he doesn't wear a shirt. Hint of sexual immorality: yes or no?

I tried to throw you with that one, but the answer is still yes.

Let's say you look at a website called Hot Chicks Gone Wild while you're at work. Hint of sexual immorality: yes or no?

Unless it's a site devoted only to fried poultry recipes, then it's still a yes.

You secretly lust after Angelina Jolie. Or Brad Pitt. Or the women on reruns of Baywatch. *Or that boy toy from One Direction. Or all of the above. Hint of sexual immorality: yes or no?*

That would be a capital-yes offense on all accounts.

Let's say you dress fashionably in tight-fitting, low-cut clothes. You can call it "stylish" or "sexy" if you want to, but you know what I'm talking about. Maybe you even try to claim that you're just showing off what God (or your plastic surgeon) gave you. Still, what do you say? *Dressing provocatively. Hint of sexual immorality: yes or no?*

Um, yes.

Now, don't misunderstand: I'm not saying that you shouldn't look great in your clothes or that you can't have plastic surgery. That's honestly none of my business. What I am saying is that *why* you wear what you wear — and why you're having work done — matters a great deal. Even if you're not doing it because you want to have sex with someone who's not your spouse, you're still doing what 1 Corinthians 8 calls becoming "a stumbling block to the weak." You're causing your brother or sister "to fall into sin." And when you do that — especially on purpose — you're not just sinning against that person. God's Word says that you're sinning against Christ. Pretty serious stuff. So dressing provocatively is definitely not keeping the marriage bed pure.

What about if you're away on a business trip without your spouse and you go out and do a little flirty (not even dirty, really) dancing? Your clothes stay on and nobody hops on top of a table at any time. It's just that you enjoy dancing and getting noticed. Plus it's good exercise. Hint of sexual immorality: yes or no?

Yes. If you want exercise, wear some baggy sweats and go for a run. You're putting yourself in a tempting place, and that's simply not wise.

You hear about some hot new book that everybody else you know is reading, say, Fifty Shades of Whatever. *Or maybe your neighborhood book group is reading it. What do you think? Should you read it too? Would that be a hint of sexual immorality?*

Fifty shades of yes, absolutely.

Let me tell you why I think that's sexual immorality. Maybe you tried to justify it, thinking it could spice up your marriage or something. But that's all it is: justifying. You know the truth: it's mommy porn. You wouldn't want your husband reading something like that, would you? Of course not. And why not? Because it's cat diarrhea. It's poison in your marriage. God's economy doesn't have fifty shades of grey. There's only black and white. There's right and wrong. If that sounds old-fashioned or extreme, I'm sorry. Just remember to think of it this way: you don't want poison in your marriage, not even "just a little."

EXTREME MEASURES

It's not just being careful not to add something that's poison; it's also avoiding those things that can easily become poisonous. Scientists call this "latent toxicity," the ability of certain substances to become poisonous under certain conditions. Sometimes this is an accumulated effect over time. Sometimes it happens under certain conditions, like pressure or temperature. Consider Paul's warning about these dangers: "Flee from sexual immorality. All other sins a person commits are outside the body, but whoever sins sexually, sins against their own body" (1 Cor. 6:18).

Does he say to flirt with sexual immorality? No! He says to flee from it. Don't just casually walk away from it. Run! Sprint! Turn tail and beat a path. Run, Forrest, run! Get away as fast as you can. Show it your taillights and don't look back.

Maybe you're thinking, "This is stupid. It's my body. I can do whatever I want with it." And you know what? That's true. If you don't follow Christ, you can do whatever you want. However, if you call yourself a Christian, then you have a different standard. You don't get to say, "It's my body. I can do whatever

I want." Paul certainly anticipated that some people might bristle about what he's saying. "Do you not know that your bodies are temples of the Holy Spirit, who is in you, whom you have received from God? You are not your own; you were bought at a price. Therefore honor God with your bodies" (1 Cor. 6:19 – 20).

Or consider this from another guy who was great at making a point — Jesus: "If your right eye causes you to stumble, gouge it out and throw it away.... If your right hand causes you to stumble, cut it off and throw it away. It is better for you to lose one part of your body than for your whole body to go into hell" (Matt. 5:29 – 30). Was he being literal? I sure hope not. If he was, there'd be a lot of one-armed cyclopses staggering around. And if you're down to just your left eye, and then *it* causes you to sin ... God help you.

I don't believe Jesus was speaking literally. I believe he was trying to communicate to us just how critical this is. He was saying that we need to deal severely with *anything* that can cause us to sin. We need to stay far away from it. We should flee from it. Or even better, don't even get close to it in the first place. It's radioactive poison.

I don't know what this would look like exactly for you, but I'll tell you some boundaries I've set in my own life. The first thing I've put in place is that I'm never alone with a woman other than my wife or daughters — under any circumstances. I won't be alone with a woman in a counseling appointment. I won't travel five minutes in the car. I won't meet with a woman for a lunch appointment. Nothing. I simply choose never to be alone with a woman who's not related to me. And I stick to that.

Another safeguard I've put in place is that all internet activity that takes place on any computer I use is monitored, whether at work or at home. The accountability software I use sends a report of every single click I make to two different men, both of whom have the authority to fire me if they notice me looking at things that could damage my integrity, my marriage, or my relationship with God.

I also have two accountability partners. I've heard some guys say, "My wife is my accountability partner." Not mine. Not only do I not think that's a good idea, honestly I think it's unfair to her. Placing that kind of a burden on her puts her in a really awkward position. Just as bad, it negatively affects the dynamics of your relationship. No, both of my accountability partners are men who will be open and honest with me. You might wonder, "Why two guys?" Because I need someone who can kick my butt if I need it, and most men can't kick my butt without help. So I found two men I could count on.

Another thing I have done is lock down my mobile phone. Remember when I pointed out the dangers of carrying internet access around with you twenty-four hours a day? Well, I have locks and restrictions set on my phone that only my accountability partners have the codes for. The phone's default browser is blocked, and even certain apps that could tempt me to look at things I should avoid. I have a special web browser installed that, although it allows me to get on the internet when I need to, filters what sites I can get to. And again, it sends reports of everything I see to my accountability partners.

MIND THE GAP

Maybe this sounds extreme to you (which doesn't bother me at all). Maybe it sounds like a lot of trouble. It is. And really inconvenient when you're trying to look up something legitimate (like fried chicken recipes or pictures of pancakes). Definitely. An obvious question might be, "So are you really *that* weak and vulnerable, Craig? That if nobody was watching, you'd look at things that were immoral or impure?"

I can honestly say the answer is, "No, not really." Right now, as I'm writing this, and as I'm thinking about these things, I'm in a really good place. My resolve is strong. I'm confident in my relationship with Christ, and everything is going really well. So why bother? Because if you are honest, you know that not every single moment of your life looks like that. Does it? Neither does mine. Sometimes I get tired. Sometimes my feelings get hurt, or I get angry, or I feel like I'm not getting everything I deserve. You know, just like everybody else. And then, in those fleeting moments of weakness, every door to temptation that I might otherwise try to turn to is completely, thoroughly, securely locked. Strong Craig of this moment is looking out for Weak Craig of those other moments.

I'd recommend you do that too. You know what your weaknesses are. Summon the courage to find solutions now, in the moments when you're strong, while you're committed to living a life of purity that will honor God and your spouse. Remain vigilant and be deliberate. The London Underground subway system is known for its motto, "Mind the Gap!" It constantly reminds commuters to be careful not to fall into the gap between the platform and the train tracks below. If we want to stay on solid ground and not fall below, then we need to have that same mindset. Do whatever you have to do right now to protect yourself later. Shore up your defenses for those moments of weakness. Block every path to impurity. Close every gap. You'll thank yourself later.

I know several married couples who have decided not to have individual Facebook accounts. They just share one instead, so the other person always knows about every interaction, eliminating even the possibility for temptation. I know lots of couples who share all of their computer and phone passwords with each other, so nothing can be hidden, and so the other person can always check anything they want to.

Some people I know decided, "We don't want anything

immoral or even questionable in our home. Let's limit how much time we spend on entertainment. We'll still watch movies and TV shows sometimes, but we'll just be a lot more selective. We'll only watch things that build us up, reinforce things we believe, enhance our family time, and strengthen our relationship with each other." Even that's not enough for some people; some simply get rid of any device or connection that could ever lead them to temptation. Some people might say that's too extreme. I'd say it's extremely wise.

Exercise godly wisdom. From this day forward, make decisions that will carry you far away from trouble. Try to look at your outward behavior from God's perspective. Would the choices you're making be pleasing to him? Could this decision you're about to make, this thing you're about to do, cause a "weaker" believer to stumble? Then choose to do what you already know is right.

SIN-SIDE OUT

If outward purity is what people can see, inward purity is just between you and God. Inward purity is what you think and feel, what's going on inside your heart.

The bottom line is even though we might try with our best human efforts to be pure outwardly, we'll still fail sometimes. That's because we simply don't have enough strength within ourselves to overcome all the temptations this world offers. Even the best solution still requires action on our part. We need to allow God to transform our hearts, so that we can live purely from the inside out and not the sin-side out.

I know sometimes it feels like you're the only person struggling to live your life the way God wants. You look at other people you know, and it seems like they just naturally do the right things. If you've ever felt like that, I hope you'll find inspiration in these words from King David: "How can a young person stay on the path of purity? By living according to your word. I seek you with all my heart; do not let me stray from your commands. I have hidden your word in my heart that I might not sin against you" (Ps. 119:9 – 11).

What a great question, especially for the world we live in, surrounded by temptations on every side. How can I stay on the path of purity? Thankfully, David answers his own question. I want you to notice three things here, three strategies David employs that you can too.

The first is simply to live according to God's Word. Look what he says: "I have hidden your word in my heart." David understands that the only way he can live according to God's Word is if he actually knows what it says. So David does what *he* can do: he takes the time to know what God's Word says. He's not just listening to other people telling him what's in God's Word; he's seeking it for himself. He's not just casually reading it either. He's hiding it in his heart, memorizing it, storing it away so he can refer to it anytime he needs to.

The next thing is that David maintains his desire for God's pure standards. Look at his urgency here: "Don't let me stray from your commands! God, I've learned what you value. Now please help me stick to those things! Guide my steps and help me stay on the path that will lead me to you."

Finally, David has taken steps toward God, then he turns to God to carry it out in his life. "I seek you with all my heart, God." What does that mean? It means he's praying. He knows what God wants from him because he's read his Word. And David's committed that that's what he wants too. Now all that's left to seal the deal is for David to maintain his relationship with God.

When we study God's Word, when we commit to live according to his purpose, and when we seek him in prayer, his Word renews our minds and transforms our hearts (Rom. 12:2). The things that used to attract us — lust and greed and selfishness and the desires of the flesh — start to repulse us. Over time, it becomes easier for us to walk a wide circle around the danger, away from the poison. We instantly recognize those things that might harm our relationship with God or damage our marriage intimacy. The very things that used to attract us start making us sick. "I don't want that! It's poison! It's cat diarrhea!" There's nothing on earth worse than Satan — and cat diarrhea.

So many people put the line in the wrong place. They say things like, "From this day forward, I'll be faithful to my wife, for as long as we both shall live. I'll never commit adultery." They don't realize that by the time they reach the sin of adultery, they will have already crossed dozens of other sin lines. Sin doesn't begin on the outside. It begins in the heart.

You see something (or someone) attractive, and you allow them to capture your attention. "Mmm, they look good." That's lust. And lust is a sin. Maybe you even take some action — just not full-blown adultery. "A body as hot as yours ought to come with a warning label!" Implying to someone else that you're available when you're not is called flirting. And it's a sin.

Maybe you don't take any action. You just see something you want, and you let your thoughts wander after it. "Yowza! I'd like to take *that* home." That's not taking every thought captive to make it obedient to Christ (2 Cor. 10:5). That's fantasizing, and it's a sin. These things are problematic because they draw the line in the wrong place.

The seeds of sin are planted long before they bloom into adultery. Jesus explained this very clearly in Matthew 5:27 – 28: "You have heard that it was said, 'You shall not commit adultery.' But I tell you that anyone who looks at a woman lustfully has already committed adultery with her in his heart.'"

Even if the act of adultery hasn't taken place yet, the problem starts the moment the seed is planted: lust. What goes on in your heart matters. While there are things you can do to get your life moving in the right direction, ultimately you can't do anything apart from the power of Christ. You have to start hiding God's Word in your heart and meditating on it. Change your behavior where you can. Take precautions. Avoid temptation. Then through the power of God's Spirit working within you, you can arrive at a state of purity you never knew was possible. But you have to start somewhere. Decide you don't want to sin against God anymore. Do whatever it takes to avoid temptation. Decide that you want to get on the path of purity. And stay on it.

WHAT'S IT WORTH?

No matter how many practical actions we take, no matter how long we remain faithfully married, maintaining purity will always be a challenge. Why? Because we're human. We're not perfect. Every one of us has sinned. We've all fallen short of God's standards (Rom. 3:23 – 24). I can't tell you how many times I've failed in this area (and countless others). And just being perfectly honest, you're going to fail sometimes too. When you do, make sure you have a strategy you can turn to for those times that you fall into temptation for sexual immorality or impurity.

We may be tempted to justify our sin — "I'm just taking care of my needs, since she's not" or "God wants me to be happy" — but that's only going to cause you to sink deeper into the quicksand of immorality. Or maybe you feel remorse, especially if you get caught by your spouse. "Wow, that was stupid. Sure wish I hadn't done that. I'm so sorry." Remorse can be dangerous because it can allow us to change our behavior temporarily — or to work extra hard next time not to get caught. We may even fool ourselves, knowing inside that we're still committed to our pleasures and desires.

The only strategy that ultimately works is honesty: transparency, accountability, confession, forgiveness. Dealing with temptation and with our failures as they happen is the only way to prevent ourselves from sinking deeper and deeper into the pit. We don't have to stay there, though — not now, not ever. Fortunately for us, we're promised that "God is faithful; he will not let you be tempted beyond what you can bear. But when you are tempted, he will also provide a way out so that you can endure it" (1 Cor. 10:13).

One of the ways God helps me to escape temptation is the result of the failure I shared at the beginning of this chapter. Amy's question to me — "Was it worth it?" — has become a mighty shield in my life. Ever since, that simple question has helped protect me, propelling me past all kinds of temptations: right before taking a second look, right before an inappropriate comment in mixed company, right before allowing my thoughts to wander, right before clicking on a questionable internet advertisement, right before freezing on a TV channel instead of turning my eyes away and clicking through.

Is this going to be worth it?

I can tell you without hesitation that my answer now is always no. And not just no, but no way ever, under any circumstances, is there any sexual thrill that would be worth compromising my integrity, hurting my relationship with God, or in any way opening a door that could hurt my wife, who's been so faithful to me. Is it worth it? No! Is it worth it? No!

If you're feeling convicted because you know there's something impure in your life, grab hold of that feeling. Let me ask you: is it worth it? No!

It's absolutely not worth it, and you know it.

No matter what that impure thing is, here's what I want you to do right now: confess it to God. Go ahead. Pray. Ask him to forgive you. First John 1:8 – 9 says: "If we claim to be without sin, we deceive ourselves and the truth is not in us. If we confess our sins, he is faithful and just and will forgive us our sins and purify us from all unrighteousness."

Seek God. Fight fair. Have fun. And by the power of Christ within you, hide his Word in your heart so you won't sin against him. Stay pure. And no matter what happens, from this day forward, never give up.

AMY'S ANGLE

Early in our relationship, Craig and I agreed that we wanted purity to be not just something that we do but something that is a part of our character, a defining quality of our relationship. God's Word tells us we should "stay away from every kind of evil" (1 Thess. 5:22 NLT). Some of the things we've done over the years to guard our purity might seem silly and insignificant to someone else. They might even seem like we were just going overboard, being ridiculous. But we take this verse seriously, and we've always tried to apply it in a literal way, being careful about the things we allow near our home and hearts.

Stay away from is an active phrase. Craig and I actively stay away from anything we think might have even the remotest possibility of leading us toward impurity, whether in our actions or thoughts. For example, we avoid certain kinds of magazines. We're careful what movies we see and what we watch on television and in other media. We don't allow culture to dictate to us what's acceptable. We protect each other from potentially dangerous relationships.

Teaching our kids how to protect themselves from things that could lead them toward sin is essential too. I believe God has blessed our family as we've heeded his Word. God's principles and commands protect our marriage from all kinds of negative consequences. These are just a few of the practical, outward things we've done, but that's only part of the equation.

The other part has to do with our personal relationship with Christ. We need to stay close to Jesus. He is the source of purity and holiness. Staying close to him sanctifies us. When we draw near to him, he gently reveals our impurities.

Because I stay close to God and have trained myself through his Word about what pleases him, when an impure thought pops into my head, I recognize it instantly. I remember that I'm committed to God and to his idea of purity, which helps me quickly reject it, replacing it with his wisdom.

We need to acknowledge that purity genuinely matters to God. He's a holy God. When he adopted us as his children, he called us to be holy too. He has set us apart to be a light in this world. Purity is truly important. What we wear matters. What we think about matters. What we look at matters. What we talk about matters. Who we choose to spend our time with matters. Purity matters to God. It matters in our marriages. We're his kids; we should look like him. We should be holy, just as he is holy.

NEVER
GIVE UP

Never confuse a single defeat with a final defeat.
— F. Scott Fitzgerald

Years ago I officiated a wedding for our close friends Scott and Shannon. As I stood before the glowing couple and all their friends and family, I talked in detail about their relationship. Scott had honored Shannon and protected her purity. Shannon had honored Scott by faithfully praying for him and encouraging him in his faith. They're two of our closest friends, and I was so excited to celebrate the commitment they were making before God, each other, and all their guests on their special day.

Midway through the ceremony, I glanced down at my carefully prepared notes and momentarily panicked. Reading ahead through the words, I saw a glaring typo. Without realizing it until that moment, I had accidentally written that the "two would be *untied*."

Of course, I had intended to write the "two would be united." Thankfully, I had the presence of mind not to read it as it was written but to correct this important detail on the fly. I probably hesitated for a moment as I made the adjustment, but I was so glad that I didn't blurt out what I had mistakenly written. Not just because I didn't want to make a goof in front of our good friends (trust me, I know the big day was not about me), but because I would've blurted out the opposite of what I had intended to communicate.

After the ceremony, I showed Amy the mistake in my notes. We both noticed that only one small letter was out of place. When the *i* was in the proper place, the word said "united." When it was in the wrong place, it read "untied."

It may sound corny, but this typo illustrates a truth. No matter what else is happening in a marriage, if "I" is not in the right place, both will become untied. If I am not fully surrendering to God and making him my One, then I can never truly love my two with his unconditional love. Depending on where the "I" lands, the marriage can be secure and firmly grounded — or it can be loose and separated.

DECIDING TO DECIDE

How about you — where do you feel like your marriage is right now? We've covered a lot of ground together in this book so far. But ultimately, this chapter may be the most important one to you if you truly want your marriage to survive and thrive. As we wrap up these five crucial decisions that can divorce-proof your marriage — seeking God, fighting fair, having fun, staying pure, and never giving up — this last one is what keeps the other four going.

And the secret to never giving up? It's easier than you think. Early in our marriage, Amy and I stumbled across a simple truth that's made all the difference. In fact, because it's so simple, it would be easy to underestimate just how powerful it can be in your life. Are you ready to hear our secret? Here it is: we decided that our marriage will be as good as we decide it will be.

The same is true for you: your marriage is as good as you've decided it will be.

We're not any better than anybody else. Don't think for a minute that just because we're in ministry we don't have problems. We have problems just like everybody else. We live in the same sin-filled world that you do. (Do you have any idea what six kids can do to a bathroom?) But we decided we would seek God together, praying together and striving to put God first. We decided we'd fight fair, always fighting toward resolution instead of toward winning, which leaves plenty of space for forgiveness and love. We decided we'd make time regularly to have fun, enjoying the gifts of marriage and friendship. We decided to keep our hearts out of trouble and to stay pure, rejecting any poison that could hurt our marriage. And of course we decided not to give up, fighting without end for the marriage God wants us to have. I hope you noticed the key words in all of those things. There are only two of them: We. Decided.

You can too! It has taken both of us working together as one. But everybody has to start somewhere. I know it's especially hard if only one of you is trying at first. But you have to keep going. You're in this relationship together. Even when it doesn't feel like it, if you're married, God has already made you one. It doesn't matter how it feels. Once God has made you one, you can't be undone. Even if you're the only one committing right now, *you* decide. You decide what kind of marriage you're going to have. Is it going to be a bad one? Or is it going to be a good one? You decide. It can be just as good as you decide.

You may be in a marriage that doesn't look like it will survive. If that's the case, I'm sorry you're there, and I want you to know that I hurt with you. You might feel like pushing back with every page you read. You might even have experienced betrayal in your marriage; you were faithful to your spouse, but your spouse wasn't faithful to you. And you know that adultery is grounds for divorce. While that's absolutely true — and most people wouldn't blame you for giving up after being betrayed — I want to remind you of another truth that's just as powerful: while adultery is grounds for divorce, it's also grounds for forgiveness.

To have the marriage that God wants you to have, I can promise you that both of you will have to do your share of forgiving. Even when forgiving may seem impossible to do, I'm thankful that all things are possible with God. All things. Even forgiving what seems unforgiveable. *Especially* forgiving what seems unforgiveable. And you will never be more like God than when you forgive.

I know you can't do anything to change your spouse. But I also know you *can* change you. You can do everything you can do to not give up. You can put yourself in the proper place, surrendering fully to God, seeking him daily, and believing for a miracle from him. You can decide to never give up. You're in a covenant, and not just with your spouse. You made a promise to God. So you hang in there and stay united, even when the enemy wants you to become untied.

Marriage means persevering. It means never giving up on each other. It means never letting your fears that your marriage might not make it turn into words or actions that you'll forever regret. It means never giving up on God's ability to do the impossible. No matter where you and your spouse find yourselves right now, I want you to consider what it means for you to run the good race together.

OPPOSITES ATTACK

Maybe there's no better way to begin thinking about how you want to finish the race together than to consider how you started. If you're married, think back to that time when you were first getting to know each other. Odds are, you were pretty different from each other. All those unusual quirks of his, that unique outlook she had on life, are what caught your attention at first — and maybe even scared you a little.

But those peculiarities were exactly what attracted you, what intrigued you enough to keep making excuses to see each other. And eventually, both of you probably started thinking, "I know we're really different from each other, but I actually think our personalities complement each other really nicely. Hmm, I wonder ..." Maybe you even eventually sensed that you were made for each other, like two halves of the same whole. Your weaknesses were her strengths. Or what she lacked, you were great at accomplishing. After all, it's like they say, "Opposites attract."

Once you got married, I'm guessing that's when the other

shoe dropped. You probably learned that while it may be true that, at least while you're dating, opposites attract — once you get married, opposites *attack!* Those little quirks and idiosyncrasies that used to be so cute and charming soon became the annoying little habits and stubborn stupidities that make you want to argue, withdraw, and wonder what you were thinking when you said, "I do."

It doesn't take long to realize that if one of you is punctual, if you feel that being on time communicates respect and love to the people you're meeting, then there's a really good chance that your mate feels … well, less so. In fact, I'd be willing to bet that your spouse approaches the whole concept of timekeeping with a lot more "creativity" than you do. Besides, they're convinced that your friends know you guys well enough that if you said 7:00, they shouldn't expect you before 7:30. In fact, it would probably even be rude for you to arrive at 7:00, because they won't be ready for you yet!

I know some couples where one partner is the saver and even carries around a printed copy of their budget. Not only have they already filled out college entry forms for kids who aren't even born yet, they've started investment accounts to pay for it. But anytime they go out to dinner with friends, their spouse is the one who tells the waiter, "Bring us your finest bottle of wine. Tonight we're celebrating the three-month anniversary of our friendship. Who wants dessert? We're buying!"

I even know one couple where one spouse likes to pretend that fat, fluffy dough balls are "pancakes," when their partner knows that God is glorified only by thin, perfectly round ones. Of course, God loves both of these people the same; it's just that he has to extend more grace and mercy to one than to the other. I'm sure you know what I'm talking about.

One way you can return to opposites attracting instead of attacking is by accepting your spouse for who they are, not who you want them to be. Your spouse may never load the dishwasher the way you would. Your spouse may never be ready on time the way you would be. Your spouse may never make pancakes the way God intended. But remember that this is not only okay, but it's part of what fascinated you about this person in the first place.

Being opposites isn't a bad thing. In fact, the truth is, if you're married to someone who's just like you, one of you is unnecessary. God knew exactly what he was doing when he brought you two opposites together. The only way iron can sharpen iron is if your differences are constantly rubbing against each other (Prov. 27:17). (And I probably don't have tell you how much fun it can be to rub your differences against each other, especially when you're belly button to belly button!)

The challenge is that we settle into a mindset and become convinced that our differences are always going to cause conflict. But that doesn't have to be true. Just because your spouse does things differently than you doesn't mean that it has to be a problem. It's just ... well, different.

If you refuse to accept your differences as the positives they are, you may find yourself sometimes trying to keep things from your spouse. For example, let's say you're the spendy one, and one time you eat lunch out by yourself, then fudge a little in the budget to cover it up. That kind of deceit can quickly evolve into a pattern, and once those "little" things start piling up, suddenly you're facing a much bigger problem.

At some point, even if you admit to your "little white lie" and ask for forgiveness — which you should — then one possible negative consequence is that now mistrust has entered the relationship. Another more serious consequence might be that both of you now have to deal with unforgiveness and maybe even long-term bitterness. There's lack of trust and resentment. Suspicion. Disappointment. Silence. And before you even realized it was happening, you wake up one day more like roommates than lovers. You may live under the same roof, but you're living separate lives.

To avoid this calcification process, you both have to make daily decisions to honor the big decisions. When you've both committed to fighting fair, then neither of you is trying to win; you're both committed to resolving the problem, not being right. When you're both committed to praying together, then you're both responsible for making this happen regularly. And when you've decided that you're never giving up, that your vows really are for a lifetime, then your daily decisions become ones of honesty and transparency, confession and forgiveness. This is the only way to keep alive those feelings you had at the beginning of your relationship.

You remember the beginning of your relationship, don't you? When you first fell in love, every romantic song on the radio made sense, every billboard along the highway "confirmed" you were destined for each other. Every time you were together, you'd do that thing where one of you holds your phone at arm's length to snap a picture of yourselves cuddling. You compulsively bought greeting cards and stuffed walruses. Then in no time at all, you're cutting up all those pictures and throwing them in the fireplace. And you're sitting in divorce court, your attorneys yelling between you, arguing bitterly over who's going to get custody of all those walruses.

Of course, it doesn't have to be like that. And certainly that's not what God wants for you. No, he knows the plans he has for you — plans to prosper you, not to harm you, plans to give you hope and a future (Jer. 29:11). But how can you see those plans fulfilled in your life? You seek God. You seek the One with your two, praying together. You fight fair. Instead of always trying to "win," you work together toward resolution. You have fun, spending quality time together face to face, side to side, and belly button to belly button. You stay pure. You don't try to see how close you can get to the line without crossing it; you flee from it, as far away as you can get. Then, once you've done all of those things, you never give up.

EMBRACE GRACE

Now, when I say you should never give up, I'm not saying you should give your spouse an all-access pass to bully you and treat you however they want. There's no such thing as having the spiritual gift of being a punching bag or a doormat. If never giving up means that you have to get a physically safe distance away before you can pursue counseling and work on your marriage, then do what you need to do to make that happen.

Also, let me take just a moment here and say that if you've already been in a marriage and it ended, I promise: today can be a new day for you. If you're in Christ, he doesn't condemn you for your past. And I won't either. Don't keep hanging on to that guilt like it's a cherished pet. Embrace grace instead. If you want to know what I'd say to you if we were face to face, just read John 8:3 – 11 and Romans 8. That's where we'd start. Then I would tell you, for whatever your part was in the loss of that relationship, accept your responsibility; then accept the mercy, grace, and forgiveness that God wants to offer you. The path that leads to your healing has to begin there.

Maybe you haven't been married, but when you look back

on past relationships, you can't help thinking, "I know I've already done a lot of things wrong. If I could go back, I'd do so many things differently." If that's you, believe me, I understand. Every one of us has things in our past that we wish we could change. But we have to be realistic: you can't change the past. Instead, we need to focus on what we *can* do: from this day forward, we should never give up. If we choose to follow Christ, then that means we serve a God who says that, with him, all things are possible (Matt. 19:26). We need to ask for forgiveness for whatever we've done wrong, then move forward and stop sinning.

Let's look at another passage from Mathew 19. In the beginning of this chapter, crowds are following Jesus around Judea, and he's healing people. Then in verse 3, some Pharisees (teachers of Hebrew law) show up with a plan to trap him with a trick question. They ask him, "Is it lawful for a man to divorce his wife for any and every reason?"

Now, before we look at Jesus' answer, I first want you to understand something about the culture of Jesus' day. It's unfortunate, and it may be hard for us to imagine this today, but during Jesus' time, not only were women not considered equals, they were treated more like property. And because they didn't really have rights, a man could simply say to his wife, "I don't want you anymore!" Then just like that, they were divorced.

So the Pharisees' plan was to try to catch Jesus off guard,

putting him on the spot with a question about Hebrew law, an area in which they just happened to be experts. But Jesus wasn't falling for it. No, instead, he shocked everybody within earshot. Jesus didn't just raise the standard a little. In fact, he didn't raise the standard at all. He annihilated the standard and introduced an entirely new one, a better one than any of them had ever considered before. Let's look at what he said, beginning in verse 4: "Haven't you read ... that at the beginning the Creator 'made them male and female,' and said, 'For this reason a man will leave his father and mother and be united to his wife, and the two will become one flesh'? So they are no longer two, but one flesh. Therefore what God has joined together, let no one separate."

These Pharisees were thinking about the law during the time of the Israelites in the wilderness, when God handed rules down to them through Moses. But Jesus took them back much farther than that, almost to the very beginning. He quoted Genesis, reminding them of the very first couple, Adam and Eve. And using those words, he pointed out that once two people get married, they're no longer two separate people, but *one*.

STUCK LIKE GLUE

Don't read more into this than is there. Jesus wasn't saying that each person gives up their rights, their personality, their individual gifts, their identity. What he was saying is that two unique individuals blend to create an entirely new being, "one flesh" together. What's more, they don't do this on their own. The new being is something that God has joined together. And when he said, "What God has joined together, let no one separate," he was explaining that the Pharisees' silly little laws and rules and guidelines don't actually apply, because man's rules can't override God's creation.

Let me use an illustration to help you picture how this works. Let's say we take two pieces of paper, one representing the husband, and the other representing the wife. Now let's superglue these two pieces of paper together, side by side, overlapping them about an inch or so, from top to bottom. They were two separate pieces of paper. But now that we've bonded them thoroughly together, they're like one, bigger piece of paper. They still have all the same attributes they had before; but now they just share everything. They were two. But now they're one.

Why do you think divorce is so painful? Because it's like trying to tear this now one piece of paper and return it back into the original two. That's not even possible anymore! No matter how carefully you try to pull them apart, you're not going to end up with the same two pieces of paper you started with. They're both going to tear. If you've been divorced, or if you've been through the pain of seeing friends or family members divorce, then you know exactly what I'm talking about. It's messy. It's destructive. And the result isn't two complete wholes; it's two tattered pieces.

I really like how I once heard Andy Stanley very simply explain this same principle. He said, "You can't un-one what God made one."

I think the reason people in our culture have such a hard time getting this is that they don't understand what marriage really is. They believe that marriage is a contract, a mutual agreement between two individual parties. But it's not. A marriage is a *covenant*. And there's a world of difference. A covenant is based on mutual commitment. A contract, on the other hand, is based on mutual distrust.

Here's what I mean: A contract is designed to limit my responsibility and increase my rights. If you and I sign a contract, it basically says that I'm in as far as you are. I commit to what I think is fair for me, and you commit to what you think is fair for you.

Before I was married, I bought my first rental home. If someone is going to rent a home from me — especially someone I don't know — then I have them sign a contract. That's because, since we don't know each other, I don't know whether I can trust them, and they don't know whether they can trust me. Our contract essentially says, "I'm in as far as you're in." If you don't do what you've agreed to do (pay your rent on time and don't damage anything), then I can have you removed from the home.

But it works both ways. For your benefit, it also says that if I don't do what I've said I'll do (make sure everything in the house is in good working order), then you have some recourse against me. We trust each other only as long as we both stick to what we said. If either one of us doesn't live up to the other's expectations, then the contract is over, and we can back out.

That's exactly how most people approach marriage. "As long as you make me happy, as long as you keep meeting my needs, as long as nothing better comes along, then we'll stick with this. But if at any point I decide you're not living up to your end of the contract, then I'm out."

But marriage is not a contract; it's a covenant. And what is a covenant? A covenant is a *permanent* relationship. Our God is a God of covenants. He makes permanent relationships with his people.

The Hebrew word that we translate as "covenant" is *beriyth* (beh-REETH). The root of this word literally means "to cut asunder," as in "to cut in two." During Old Testament times, for two parties to enter into a binding agreement, it required a blood sacrifice. They would slice a bull in half, and then both of them would walk back and forth through the inside of the bull seven times. In this ritual, they were essentially saying, "If I break my part of this covenant, may what happened to this bull happen to me." Entering into a covenant was serious business.

Also during Old Testament times, when a couple got married, a part of their marriage ceremony was that they would stand before a representative of God, who would take the groom's hand and cut it with a sharp blade until it began to bleed. The priest then took the bride's hand and did the same thing to her. Then he placed their hands together so that their blood mixed. Why? Because Leviticus 17:14 says, "The life of every creature is in its blood." To them, as they mingled their blood, they mingled their lives.

Finally, the priest tied a fancy cord around their still-clasped hands, symbolizing for the witnesses, including God, that they were no longer two, but one. "What God has joined together, let no one separate." They were joined together, "no longer two, but one flesh."

OUT OF GAS

Because of the ceremony, because of the significance of what you're doing when you get married, I always encourage couples to be married by a Christian pastor if it's at all possible. If you were already married by a justice of the peace, certainly don't feel any condemnation. But if you ever decide you'd like to renew your vows, I'd urge you to seriously consider standing before a minister and answering to God. When Amy and I did that, do you think it went something like the following?

"Now, Craig. Do you take Amy to be your lawfully wedded wife, to have and to hold, from this day forward, as long as she's always getting better (even if you get worse), as long as she's healthy (and she takes good care of you when you're sick), preferably for richer (although not necessarily for poorer), forsaking all others (who are not as attractive as she is)? Do you pledge to be faithful to her (as long as she makes you happy)? Will you remain with her (as long as she holds up her end of the bargain)? Will you commit to stay in the marriage (as long as nobody better comes along)?"

Of course that's not what we said! Marriage is for better or worse, in sickness and in health, for richer or poorer, forsaking all others, from this day forward, for as long as you both shall live. There's no end date on a marriage. A covenant can end only when one of the parties dies. A contract can have an end date. For example, if you commit to rent a house from me for twelve months, one year from now we're through. But a covenant is until death do us part, so help me, God!

No matter how tough circumstances become, or how much your feelings change, the covenant of marriage remains in place. During the height of Billy Graham's ministry, the world-renowned evangelist frequently had to travel. In fact, it wasn't uncommon for him to be on the road for months at a time, conducting crusades and speaking at various events. That means that it often fell to Billy's wife, Ruth Graham, to raise their children by herself, and to care for their home while he was gone. I can guarantee you it was just as hard for her then as it would be for one of us today. Single parenting is tough. Well, several years ago, a reporter asked Ruth if she had ever considered divorcing Billy during their more than sixty years of marriage together. At the time, Ruth said, "No, I never considered divorcing Billy. I did consider murdering him at times, but never divorce!"

When we make a covenant before God, we need to keep it, no matter what. Of course, being a pastor, I've probably heard most of the reasons people give for why they just don't think they can go on living with their spouse anymore:

"I'm just not happy."

"I don't trust him."

"She's changed. She's not the same person I married years ago."

And then of course there's that timeless classic: "I just don't love them anymore."

Deciding you should get divorced because you've run out of love is like deciding you should sell your car because it has run out of gas. No reasonable person would ever do that. You simply put more gas in your car and go on. If your marriage "love low" light comes on, pull over and start putting love back into your marriage. Once you've filled it back up, then you can go on.

SOWING LESSONS

I know it's not easy. I get it. But in those times when you feel you don't have any more love, don't have any more forgiveness, don't have any more grace, when you feel like you've already done everything you can, that's when seeking God really pays off. God has to be your source. Loving isn't something God *does*; it's who he *is*. First John 4:8 says that "God is love." When you don't have any love left to give, let him love through you. You can extend God's forgiveness and grace through your life. But you have to go to him to get more, to refill your tank.

If you want to call yourself a Christian, then you have to get a handle on this. You cannot say, "I love God, but I hate my spouse." I'll tell you why. In that same chapter, 1 John 4:20 says, "Whoever claims to love God yet hates a brother or sister is a liar. For whoever does not love their brother and sister, whom they have seen, cannot love God, whom they have not seen." If you're a Christian and your spouse is a Christian, then Scripture makes it clear: you can't say you love God but you don't love your spouse. Believe me, I understand that it can be hard, especially when things haven't been going well between you. But if you love God, then you'll seek him, no matter how hard it is. Give God the opportunity to do what you may not have the strength to do yourself: let him continue to love through you.

What does this look like in your life? How can you apply what I'm telling you? Let's say you feel like you've been trying to love, but you just haven't been getting anywhere. In God's economy (and therefore in your marriage) you reap what you sow. No one gets around this principle. Whether you're married or not, this is a foundational teaching that affects absolutely every relationship in your life. Galatians 6:7 – 9 says this: "Do not be deceived: God cannot be mocked. A man reaps what he sows. Whoever sows to please their flesh, from the flesh will reap destruction; whoever sows to please the Spirit, from the Spirit will reap eternal life. Let us not become weary in doing good, for at the proper time we will reap a harvest if we do not give up."

One reason that we stay pure is because we don't want to "sow to please our flesh" — that is, our sinful nature. But when we "sow to please the Spirit" (by constantly seeking God through prayer), then from his Spirit we'll reap eternal life. Even as Paul was writing this, he had to know how hard it was going to be for people to do it. How do I know that? Because right after he said it, he encouraged us not to give up. The only way we get the benefit, the only way we reap the harvest, is if we don't give up.

When you're applying this to your marriage, there are two principles you need to understand. The first is that you will always reap whatever you sow. If you plant an apple seed in the ground, what's going to grow from that? An orange tree? Of course not! Planting and cultivating apple seeds yields apple trees. You reap what you sow.

When someone smiles at you, what do you usually do in response? You smile right back. You reap what you sow.

When someone yells at you angrily, how are you most likely to respond? It's probably going to make you angry and defensive, isn't it? You reap what you sow.

That's exactly why, when you're married, you should constantly try to show grace and compassion and thoughtfulness to your spouse. If you can do that, what are you likely to get back? Grace and compassion and thoughtfulness. You reap what you sow.

But if you're constantly complaining and criticizing your spouse, what are you going to get back? They're going to complain right back. They're going to get angry and defensive, and the odds are that, even if they're in the wrong, they'll start trying to justify their behavior to you. That's because the harvest you get depends on the seeds you plant. You reap what you sow.

NO EXCUSES

As we wrap up talking about what it takes to build a really strong marriage, there's one last thing I want to be sure we address. I'm not naive. I understand that all of these things we've been talking about take a lot of work to make them happen. Relationships are hard to get right. They require your constant attention and involvement.

So what about those of you who are thinking, "Craig, those things sound all well and good, and maybe they'd even work for some people. But not for me. I just don't feel it. I've already done everything I'm going to do. I don't feel like trying to be nice anymore. I don't feel like forgiving. I don't feel like showing grace. I don't feel like praying. I don't feel like committing to all that work. I don't feel like staying married. I just don't feel like it. So I'm not going to."

Right? I mean, I've heard these explanations from couples before. And I'll offer you the same advice I gave them. What I'm about to say might come across as harsh. I don't mean it that way. I'm going to speak directly only because I really care and believe God wants to give you a marriage better than you can imagine. Are you ready? Here it is:

When someone says they won't try because they don't feel like it, I say, "Are you kidding me?! You sound like a whiny five-year-old kid! In what other area of your life can you make that excuse — 'I just don't *feel* like it' — and get away with it?" Let's look at a few examples:

"I'm tired of working. I just don't feel like working anymore. So I'm not going to work this year."

Have you ever heard that old saying, "If you don't work, you don't eat"? Did you ever wonder where it came from? It's from the Bible (2 Thess. 3:10).

"I'm so tired of taking care of my kids. I just don't feel like doing it anymore. It seems like the baby's crying all the time, and everybody always needs something. I just don't want to be a parent anymore."

But that's not really an option, is it? No. So what do you do? You take a deep breath, you suck it up, you overcome those feelings, and you take care of your kids.

"I'm so sick of taxes. I don't feel like paying them anymore. I think I'm just going to stop paying my taxes."

Hmm. I wonder how that's going to go. That's probably not going to work out for you, at least not for long, right? So what do you do? Regardless of how you feel, you do what's right. You just put on your big kid pants, you get over your feelings, you behave like an adult, and you do the right thing.

When I tell you not to give up on your marriage, I'm not telling you that you need to just clench your teeth and take it, that you're just going to suffer in a bad marriage for the rest of your life but, bless God, you're staying married, even if it's a forty-year nightmare.

That's not what I'm saying at all. What I *am* telling you is that you're going to reap whatever you sow. I'm convinced, first through God's Word and then through years of personal experience, that if you'll start pouring love and forgiveness and grace and honor and respect back into your marriage — and you won't give up — then eventually you're going to reap the harvest from that. Honestly, it may take some time to overcome all the toxicity you've been pouring into it up until now. But if you keep after it, eventually, at the proper time, you'll reap a harvest.

What will your harvest look like? I honestly can't say. Your ideal harvest may look different than mine. But I can sure give you some ideas:

If you'll get yourself back in the game ...

If you'll keep seeking God, fighting fair, having fun, staying pure, and never giving up ...

If you'll continue to make God your One and earnestly seek him with your two ...

If you'll forgive when you've been hurt and confess your sins when you need to ...

If you'll work through issues together instead of letting them build up ...

If you'll swallow your pride and get Christ-centered counseling when you need it ...

If you'll surround yourself with wise, godly friends ...

If you'll reach out for help, instead of always trying to figure everything out yourself ...

If you'll accept that sometimes you're going to face setbacks but refuse to let those stop you ...

If you'll accept that your marriage isn't a contract but a covenant before a Holy God ...

Then God will honor your commitment and your work. You'll build a testimony. You'll be able to look back on this time as the moment when everything turned around for you. You'll be able to share with others about how distant you were from each other and from God, but how he drew you both closer to him and to each other.

If you've been selfish and resentful, God will change your heart. If you haven't been the husband you could have been, God can transform you into a man after his own heart. If you haven't been the wife you hoped to be, by the power of his Holy Spirit, you can become a mighty woman of God, grateful and amazed at the life he's blessed you with.

Your friends won't look at you the same. They'll envy what you have, and they'll want it too. You'll be an unshakeable model of integrity. People you work with will be able to see that you're not the same — you're not like you were before, and you're not like anybody else either. Your children will be proud of you. They'll look up to you and value your wise counsel. You'll build a legacy that honors God and spans generations.

It starts now.

It starts today.

Decide.

No matter what has happened in the past, from this day forward, you will:

Seek God.

Fight fair.

Have fun.

Stay pure.

And *never* give up.

AMY'S ANGLE

Craig's already told you so much about not giving up, and I hope you're really taking it to heart. Your marriage will work best if you're both committed to one another. Way back at the beginning of our marriage, I remember Craig and I came across a quote from advice columnist Ann Landers, and it has meant so much to us. She said, "Neglect the whole world before you neglect each other." What fantastic advice!

Time together is essential. Work on going in the same direction as each other. Relational drift happens if we don't commit to regularly sharing our lives as a couple. I know you can't be together twenty-four hours a day. We all get swamped with work and pre-occupied with the never-ceasing demands of life. But do whatever you have to do to keep in touch and stay on the same page, every day. Neglect is not part of a healthy marriage. Don't allow distractions to stop you from engaging with your spouse. Ask God to show you ways to pursue them. Seek God first and make your spouse your priority human relationship.

One thing I recommend that people do — and I

honestly try to do this really diligently for Craig—is to pray daily for your spouse.

Besides the obvious thing (that you're asking God to work through your spouse's life), thinking about them in this way helps you keep on their side. If your marriage relationship has slipped to the point where you feel like your spouse is your enemy, then you should pray for them all the more. Jesus tells us in Luke 6:28 that we should bless those who curse us and pray for those who mistreat us. Praying for them is the best thing you can do.

Connecting to God in prayer is essential for our hearts too. Pride is a huge marital vice. Many times, what we're missing in our relationships is humility. I can get so caught up in wanting to be right. But pride is death to intimacy. It's only when I humble myself and seek peace that endearing affection can grow. I need to humbly keep offering Craig the same grace and mercy that God has lavishly given to me.

Jesus told us in Matthew 19:26 that with God all things are possible. Cling to this truth as you continually pursue and humbly pray for your spouse.

Never give up on what God can do with your marriage.

Never.

AS LONG AS YOU BOTH SHALL LIVE

My good intentions don't always convert to good actions, so I want to thank you for finishing this book. I can't tell you how many books I start reading but don't finish. The fact that you read to the end shows that you really care about honoring God and having a marriage that goes the distance. I pray that you have been encouraged by what you've read.

As I reflect over my past, my mistakes, my sins, I have to admit that I'm completely undeserving to have a good, God-honoring marriage. (Amy would tell you the same thing about herself.) Before I was a Christian, I cheated on every girlfriend I ever had — every single one. Amy is the only girl that I've ever been faithful to. In fact, even as a young Christian, I wondered if I had what it took to be a faithful, godly husband. And the truth is I didn't. The same is true today. I really don't have what it takes. That's why I love the phrase most couples say in their wedding vows: "I promise to be faithful to my spouse as long as we both shall live, *so help me, God.*"

I need God in order to love another person unconditionally. I need his help to overlook offenses. I need his help to guard myself against all the temptations that lurk around every corner. I need his help to become more like Christ so I can lay down my life for Amy. Without him, our marriage wouldn't be anything special. Odds are it would end badly, just like so many do. But by making him our One, he makes us one. And no one can un-one what God makes one.

The same can be true for you. You can have the marriage God wants you to have. But you can't have it without God's help.

No matter what's happened in your past, this is a new day. A new chance. A new beginning.

From this day forward, things can be different.

From this day forward, you can find healing.

From this day forward, you can be more intimate.

From this day forward, you can truly forgive as you've been forgiven.

From this day forward, you can become closer to your spouse than you've ever been before.

Just remember: the past is the past. You can't change it. But God can change your future. He can take what the enemy meant for evil and use it for good. What could have destroyed your marriage, God can use to make you stronger, closer, and give you an unbreakable bond.

It might feel like you have too much to overcome. You don't.

It might seem like the damage is too great to be repaired. It's not.

You might not think you have what it takes. You don't. But God does.

Don't let this be complicated. It doesn't have to be. Keep your marriage simple, focused, and Christ-centered.

No matter what's happened before, you will seek the One with your two. He is your source. Your strength. Your sustainer.

You will fight fair. You don't fight *for* victory; you fight *from* the victory God has given you. Together you will find resolution. And your differences won't divide you; they'll strengthen you.

You will enjoy each other like you once did, having fun the way God intended. Face to face. Side to side. Belly button to belly button.

You will reject the poisons of impurity, and you'll stay pure. You've resolved that even just a moment of impurity is not worth it. Not even a hint.

And because God never gave up on you, you will never give up on him or on your marriage.

From this day forward.

Acknowledgments

We would like to express our deepest gratitude to all our friends who helped make this book possible.

Dudley Delffs. Every project with you is a blessing to do. Not only are you an amazing editor, but you are an even better friend.

David Morris, Tom Dean, John Raymond, Brian Phipps, and the whole team at Zondervan. Your heart to honor Christ with the written word is why we love partnering with you most.

Tom Winters. Thanks for believing in us and being a valuable part of our church family.

Brannon Golden. Every project we've done is better because of you. God has given you an amazing gift. Thanks for sharing it with us.

Lori Tapp, Adrianne Manning, Stephanie Pok. You are the best support team in the world. We love you and thank God for you.

Catie, Mandy, Anna, Sam, Stephen, Joy. We could not be more proud of your passion to serve Christ. We are thankful for every day with you.

Fight

Winning the Battles
That Matter Most

Craig Groeschel

Author and pastor Craig Groeschel helps
you uncover who you really are—a powerful
man with the heart of a warrior. With God's
help, you'll find strength to fight the battles
you know you must win: the ones that determine the state of your
heart, the quality of your marriage, and the spiritual health of those
you love most.

Craig examines the life of Samson—a strong man with glaring weaknesses. Like many men, Samson taunted his enemy and rationalized
his sins. The good news is God's grace is greater than your worst sin.
By looking at Samson's life, you'll learn to defeat the demons that
make strong men weak. You'll tap into a strength you never knew was
possible. You'll become who God made you to be—a man who knows
how to fight for what's right.

Don't just fight like a man. Fight like a man of God.

For God's Sake ... FIGHT

Available in stores and online!

Fight Study Guide

Winning the Battles That Matter Most

Craig Groeschel

In *Fight*, a five-session, video-based small-group Bible study, pastor and bestselling author Craig Groeschel explores the life of Samson, helping you uncover who you really are—a man created with a warrior's heart in the image of God—and how to stand up and fight for what's right.

Find the strength to fight the battles you know you need to fight—the ones that determine the state of your heart, the quality of your marriage, and the spiritual health of your family. The battles that make you dependent on God as the source of your strength. The battles that make you come alive.

Craig looks at the life of Samson, showing how much we have in common with this guy. Things didn't work out so well for him in the end. But by looking at his life, you'll learn how to defeat the demons that make strong men weak. You'll become who God made you to be—a man who knows how to fight for what's right.

Learn how to fight with faith, with prayer, and with the Word of God. Then, when your enemy begins to attack, fight for the righteous cause that God gave you. Draw a line in the sand. Make your enemy pay. Make sure he gets the message. Don't cross a warrior. Don't mess with this man of God. Come out fighting.

And don't show up for this fight unarmed.

Use the weapons God gave you, and you'll win. Can you feel it? It's inside you.

It's time to fight like a man.

Designed for use with the *Fight* DVD (sold separately).

Altar Ego

Becoming Who God Says You Are

Craig Groeschel

You are NOT who you think you are. In fact, according to bestselling author Craig Groeschel, you need to take your idea of your own identity, lay it down on the altar, and sacrifice it. Give it to God. Offer it up.

Why? Because you are who GOD says you are. And until you've sacrificed your broken concept of your identity, you won't become who you are meant to be.

When we place our false labels and self-deception on the altar of God's truth, we discover who we really are as his sons and daughters. Instead of an outward-driven, approval-based ego, we learn to live with an "altar" ego, God's vision of who we are becoming.

Discover how to trade in your broken ego and unleash your altar ego to become a living sacrifice. Once we know our true identity and are growing in Christlike character, then we can behave accordingly, with bold behavior, bold prayers, bold words, and bold obedience.

Altar Ego reveals who God says you are, and then calls you to live up to it.

Small Group Curriculum Also Available:
• 5-Session DVD
• Study Guide
• Study Guide with DVD

Available in stores and online!